David Li

Jason Q. Ng is a 2013 Google Policy Fellow at the University of Toronto's Citizen Lab and a research consultant for *China Digital Times*. His work has been featured in *Le Monde*, the *Huffington Post*, the *Next Web*, *Asia Pacific Forum*, and *Shanghaiist*. He writes regularly on China for *Waging Nonviolence*. He lives in New Jersey.

BLOCKED ON WEIBO

BLOCKED ON WEIBO

WHAT GETS SUPPRESSED ON CHINA'S VERSION OF TWITTER (AND WHY)

JASON Q. NG

THE NEW PRESS

NEW YORK
LONDON

Requests for permission to reproduce selections from this book should be mailed to:
Permissions Department, The New Press, 38 Greene Street, New York, NY 10013.

Published in the United States by The New Press, New York, 2013
Distributed by Perseus Distribution

LIBRARY OF CONGRESS CATALOGING-IN-PUBLICATION DATA

Ng, Jason Q., 1984-
 Blocked on weibo : what gets suppressed on China's version of Twitter (and why) /
Jason Q. Ng.
    pages cm
 Includes bibliographical references.
 ISBN 978-1-59558-871-5 (pbk. : alk. paper) -- ISBN 978-1-59558-885-2
(e-book) 1. Censorship--China. 2. Internet searching--China. 3.Internet--Censorship--
China. 4. Internet--Political aspects--China. 5. Freedom of information--China. I. Title.
 Z658.C6.N42 2013
 363.310951--dc23
                              2013010628

The New Press publishes books that promote and enrich public discussion and understanding of the issues vital to our democracy and to a more equitable world. These books
are made possible by the enthusiasm of our readers; the support of a committed group of
donors, large and small; the collaboration of our many partners in the independent media
and the not-for-profit sector; booksellers, who often hand-sell New Press books; librarians;
and above all by our authors.

www.thenewpress.com

Book design and composition by Bookbright Media
This book was set in Times New Roman, PT Sans, and Adobe Kaiti

Printed in the United States of America

10 9 8 7 6 5 4 3 2 1

For Dad, who would've been amused by this

CONTENTS

aphrodisiac, foot fetish, nude photograph, without hair, panty hose, people eat people, lesbian, seven deadly sins, incest, marijuana, Demerol, roofied, inject monument, Bloomberg, CAPTCHA, conquered nation, Wöhler / Villar, supplement, black angel, color of leopard

INTRODUCTION

This project started with an image. No, it wasn't the famed image of the "tank man" staring down a column of armored vehicles outside Tiananmen Square in Beijing. Nor was it an image of any specific dissident act or a photo of protesters. In fact, this image wasn't meant to be artistic at all. But in the stark way it communicates its contents, one might even call it poetic.

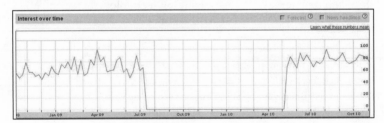

The above graph shows the volume of online search activity, as tracked by Google, originating from the northwestern Chinese province of Xinjiang.[1] While it may not be as vivid as the tank man photo, the above figure certainly conveys a different, powerful

---

1. You can generate this graph yourself: www.google.com/trends/explore#q=a&geo =CN-65&date=10/2008%2025m&cmpt=q. If you're skeptical of Google's data, you can replicate similar results of a large gap in search activity in Xinjiang using China's largest search engine, Baidu: index.baidu.com/main/word.php?type =1&area=926&time=200901-201101&word=q. Thank you to Pierre F. Landry for introducing me to this graph.

message; even someone without any knowledge of how the Internet works can look at this chart and conclude, "Looks like somebody turned something off." And indeed, for roughly ten months, from July 2009 to May 2010, web access was essentially shut down in the entire province of Xinjiang after rioting and protests erupted there.[2] The graph lays bare the ability of a government to control what was thought to be uncontrollable: the Internet.

Inspired by this graph and by the impressive attempts of *China Digital Times*'s website to track banned words across various Chinese online services,[3] I concocted a scheme to systematically uncover as many blocked words as I could on Sina Weibo, China's most important social media website. I designed a computer script to use 700,000 Chinese Wikipedia titles[4] as search terms on Weibo to see what would happen. For three months, the script performed searches on Weibo and recorded whether any of the terms were reported to be censored. I've collected and annotated more than 150 of those banned terms in this book. In hypothesizing about why they might be blocked, *Blocked on Weibo* is designed to offer an engaging and informative introduction to Chinese history, culture, and politics as well as a way to think about issues of media, censorship, and democracy in a fast-changing technological world. What

---

2. According to state media, in late June 2009, a Chinese Han factory worker (Han being the majority ethnic group in China) in Shaohuan City, Guangdong Province, falsely alleged that six Uyghur men had raped a woman. Commentators surmised that the antagonism might have arisen from the perception that Uyghurs, who mostly hail from the province of Xinjiang, thousands of miles away, are stealing local jobs by working for lower wages. Whatever the reason, a bloody fight along ethnic lines took place in and around the toy factory, with at least two Uyghur men killed. Demonstrations demanding a full investigation into their deaths were planned in the capital city of Ürümqi in their home province in Xinjiang, and violent confrontations broke out between protesters and police on July 5. Who triggered the violence and whether the protest was organized by overseas Uyghur separatist groups (as Chinese authorities claim) are disputed matters. Thousands took to the streets, several hundred people were killed, and hundreds were detained. Among the government reactions to prevent further spread of the protests and to hinder organizers was to cut off cell phone service and Internet access in the region.

3. "敏感词库," *China Digital Times*, accessed December 17, 2012, chinadigitaltimes .net/space/敏感词库.

4. You can download them for yourself here: dumps.wikimedia.org/zhwiki.

this book does not provide is a scathing critique of China's Internet policies, a position I feel is better left to those who are more directly connected to, more knowledgeable of, and more affected by the situation, and I hope readers don't automatically assume this book is a rant against China. Rather, *Blocked on Weibo* shares an affinity with the mission statement of the now defunct *Tunnel*, an underground mainland Chinese electronic magazine, which once wrote,

> Instead of indulging in the talk of noble causes and great aspirations, it is a better idea to quietly and patiently study the details of the technology. If we have turned our inaugural statement into a technical manual, it is because we are trying to practice this idea. It may be easier for us to approach our shared dream of freedom and democracy through the sideways of technical details than the public square of seething emotions.[5]

Thus, by impartially examining these various censored keywords, we may perhaps see more clearly the sorts of challenges facing Chinese officials, companies, and Internet users as they confront and utilize social media. If nothing else, you'll get a little Chinese history lesson from each word's explanation.

Weibo is run by a private company, Sina, which is legally responsible for the content that users upload to the website. Weibo (微博)[6] is a general term for microblogging—literally, "tiny blog"—representing a whole host of Twitter-like websites in China. However, Weibo has become synonymous with the most active microblogging site, Sina Weibo. Sina wasn't the first company to launch a weibo service in China, but it is by far the most significant such site in China today. The site is not just a virtual playground for people to share jokes and photos[7] of their pets with

---

5. Guobin Yang, *The Power of the Internet in China* (New York: Columbia University Press, 2010), 92.

6. Weibo (*Wēibó* in pinyin) is pronounced "way-baw" ("baw" as in the word "bawl").

7. A 2011 analysis from HP Labs showed that Weibo users had a propensity for sharing jokes and images, especially via retweets (that is, by reposting another user's original message to their own microblog). Louis Yu, Sitaram Asur, and Bernardo A. Huberman, "What Trends in Chinese Social Media," 5th SNA-KDD Workshop '11, August 21, 2011.

stuffed animals,[8] but also an avenue used to organize protests and share grievances.[9]

Weibo may have started as a Twitter clone, and for Western readers unfamiliar with the service it's still probably simplest to talk about it as such. But in recent years, Weibo has developed a number of features that Twitter doesn't have, including semi-threaded comments, events, polls, games, Facebook-like apps, instant messaging, and community portals. Aided by China's banning of Twitter and the addition of these attractive features, Sina Weibo has become the undisputed first source for real-time information in China, with over 350 million registered accounts. Whenever I refer to Weibo in this book, I am referring to Sina's weibo service (as opposed to its primary competitor, Tencent, and Tencent's weibo site). Chinese websites are required by law to monitor themselves and remove any material that is deemed offensive by the government. Sina Weibo is allowed in China, whereas Facebook and Twitter are not, because Sina, like all major Chinese Internet websites, is willing to censor the site's content.

The websites can do this in a number of ways, including deleting individual posts—a manpower-intensive task that both infuriates and exasperates users. In many ways, one of the easiest and most flexible ways to censor the flow of information on a site, however, is to block users from searching for specific terms. In addition to returning zero results for these sensitive keywords, Weibo notes when it has in fact blocked your search, helpfully displaying an error message: "根据相关法律法规和政策, [the blocked keyword] 搜索结果未予显示" ("According to relevant laws, regulations and policies, search results for [the blocked keyword] cannot be displayed"). Thus, one is aware when search results are blocked, unlike other instances when the so-called Great Firewall and Golden Shield may leave a user ignorant that his connection and searches are being filtered or degraded.

---

8. 最爱摆弄家 (hotvote), "小动物本尊和他们毛绒绒的可爱分身," Sina Weibo, October 25, 2012, weibo.com/1851825901/z29CShKTy.

9. Rachel Lu, "Dramatic Photos—NIMBY Protest Turns Bloody in Western China," *Tea Leaf Nation*, July 3, 2012, www.tealeafnation.com/2012/07/dramatic-photos -nimby-protest-turns-bloody-in-western-china.

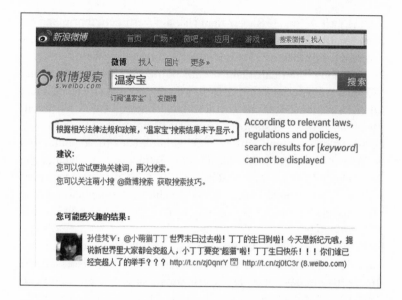

Blocked on Weibo documents these sensitive words and posits why each one might be censored. However, this book is not a definitive list of words banned in China; it is merely what one website—albeit the most important social media website in China—does not allow its users to search for on its site. The hope with this project is to make clear that censorship in China is a complex and nuanced issue,[10] and in each entry I try to provide the proper context to explain why a word might be singled out for censorship. Sometimes the reason seems to be historical; sometimes it is very contemporary. Sometimes I'm just plain mystified. Though some of these sensitive words were no doubt ordered to be placed on Weibo's blacklist by government officials, many others are here due to self-censorship

---

10. China, like any country, has its flaws, but one can't merely reduce the issue of censorship, online culture, and Chinese culture described in this book to "Hey, look at those crazy Chinese." And in China's defense, based on the political upheaval and social turmoil taking place all across the world, especially in developing nations, it may have a legitimate case for wanting to control its transition to a more open society (if that is indeed the goal). Can it continue to do so in the heavy-handed manner that it does so today? Probably not. But automatically to declare any Internet regulation evil without considering IRL ("in real life") politics and social issues is unfair to the countries that have to grapple with such complicated issues.

on the part of Sina.[11] Rather than risk a government reprimand for accidentally letting offensive material slip through, the company overcensors, blocking even seemingly innocent keywords.

The noted political scientist Gary King says that research into China's online censorship "exposes an extraordinarily rich source of information about the Chinese government's interests, intentions, and goals—a subject of long-standing interest to the scholarly and policy communities."[12] This book tries to do something similar: by tracking the various words blocked on Weibo, we might be able to get a general sense of what is considered a sensitive topic to Chinese authorities and achieve a more nuanced understanding of the politics at play in Chinese social media—and society—today.[13]

Over the past decade, many smart people have taken up this task—looking into how and what exactly China censors on the Internet—among them David Bamman and his colleagues at

---

11. Though seemingly oxymoronic, the self-censorship is indeed "enforced," that is, companies are held accountable if their quasi-voluntary regulatory efforts do not meet the Chinese Communist Party's strict (but vague) standards; for instance, Tencent's and Sina's commenting features on their weibo sites were disabled in the aftermath of the Bo Xilai scandal in March 2012. Xinhua, China's official news agency, quoted an unnamed State Internet Information Office spokesman who confirmed the shutdown was a punishment: "The SIIO spokesman also said with regard to a number of rumors having appeared on weibo.com [Sina Weibo] and t.qq.com [Tencent Weibo], the two popular microblogging sites have been 'criticized and punished accordingly' by Internet information administration authorities in Beijing and Guangdong respectively" ("China's Major Microblogs Suspend Comment Function to 'Clean Up Rumors,'" Xinhua, March 31, 2012, news.xinhuanet.com/english/china /2012-03/31/c_131500416.htm).

12. Gary King, Jennifer Pan, and Margaret E. Roberts, "How Censorship in China Allows Government Criticism but Silences Collective Expression," *American Political Science Review*, in press, gking.harvard.edu/gking/publications/how -censorship-china-allows-government-criticism-silences-collective-expression.

13. David Bamman and his colleagues confirmed that they could identify the sensitive words that caused certain messages to be deleted at much higher rates than typical. Those sensitive words were found to be blocked on Weibo's search engine at a much higher rate as well, verifying that a link exists between this "hard" censorship (the search blocks that Weibo tells the user about) and "soft" censorship (the posts that are covertly deleted), both of which are connected to these sensitive terms.

Carnegie Mellon University,[14] the developers of Weiboscope[15] and other researchers at the University of Hong Kong,[16] Jedidiah R. Crandall at the University of New Mexico,[17] Xiao Qiang and *China Digital Times*,[18] Martin Johnson and GreatFire.org, Jonathan Zittrain and his colleagues at Harvard's Berkman Center,[19] the aforementioned Gary King, and many others, and I have often extrapolated from their insights. But, of course, any conclusions I reach may well be off base, and all errors are my own.[20]

Out of the roughly 700,000 terms I searched, I came up with more than 1,000 blocked keywords, roughly 500 of which were

14. David Bamman, Brendan O'Connor, and Noah A. Smith, "Censorship and Deletion Practices in Chinese Social Media," *First Monday*, March 5, 2012, firstmonday.org/htbin/cgiwrap/bin/ojs/index.php/fm/article/view/3943/3169.

15. King-wa Fu, CH Chan, and Michael Chau, "Assessing Censorship on Microblogs in China," *IEEE Internet Computing*, February 11, 2013, doi.ieeecomputersociety.org/10.1109/MIC.2013.28.

16. Cedric Sam, YY Chan, David Bandurski, and King-wa Fu, "A Fully Automated Method to Catch and Characterize Deleted Posts on Sina and Tencent Weibo," YouTube, presented May 21, 2012, at 10th Annual Chinese Internet Research Conference at University of Southern California, www.youtube.com/watch?v=rzZytcOn1Kc.

17. Jedidiah Crandall, Daniel Zinn, Michael Byrd, Earl Barr, and Rich East, "ConceptDoppler, a Weather Tracker for Internet," 14th ACM Conference on Computer and Communications Security, November 2007, www.csd.uoc.gr/~hy558/papers/conceptdoppler.pdf; Jong Chun Park and Jedidiah R. Crandall, "Empirical Study of a National-Scale Distributed Intrusion Detection System: Backbone-Level Filtering of HTML Responses in China," International Conference on Distributed Computing Systems, June 2010, www.cs.unm.edu/~crandall/icdcs2010.pdf; Tao Zhu, David Phipps, Adam Pridgen, Jedidiah R. Crandall, and Dan S. Wallach, "The Velocity of Censorship: High-Fidelity Detection of Microblog Post Deletions," arXiv.org, March 4, 2013, arxiv.org/abs/1303.0597.

18. "新浪微博搜索敏感词列表 (更新中) Sensitive Sina Weibo Search Terms (Updating)," *China Digital Times*, Google Docs, accessed December 17, 2012, docs.google.com/spreadsheet/ccc?key=0Aqe87wrWj9w_dFpJWjZoM19BNkFfV2JrWSlpMEtYcEE#gid=0.

19. Jonathan Zittrain and Benjamin Edelman, "Empirical Analysis of Internet Filtering in China," Berkman Center for Internet & Society, March 20, 2003, cyber.law.harvard.edu/filtering/china.

20. If you have your own reasoned conjectures or spot a mistake in my entries, feel free to contact me on Twitter @jasonqng or via my website: blockedonweibo.com.

unique. Of those 500 unique blocked words, I've selected over 150 terms, which cover a range of topics and moments in Chinese history, and organized them thematically in the book. The largest share of the blocked words are names of people, the majority of whom are Communist Party members—protection from criticism on Weibo seems to be a perk for rising up the ranks—while dissidents and people caught up in scandals or crimes make up the rest of the names. Some of the other words I uncovered are equally unsurprising—for instance, political terms such as 六四 (64, short for June 4, 1989, the day of the crackdown in Tiananmen Square; see student leader, page 152) and 反共 (anti-Communism; see Communist dog, page 198). Others, such as 乱伦 (incest, page 83), 暴露狂 (exhibitionism; see dew point, page 74), and 吹箫 (blowing a flute, slang for blow job; see one-night stand, page 66), spoke to social mores and topics that were sensitive for prurient reasons. A few terms, such as 伊斯兰 (Islam, page 190) and 同性爱 (homosexuality; see lesbian, page 81), were surprising in their reactionary nature. And finally, some words, such as 黄色 (yellow, slang for something pornographic; see rare beauty, page 69, note 8), seemed to border on the ridiculous[21]—until one comes to understand the context and the subsurface significance of the word.When I say "banned" or "censored" on Weibo in this book, I generally mean that the word is "blocked" in the search function of the site. Users can post just about anything they want to the site. But many words subsequently yield no results when they are searched for, such as 温家宝 (Wen Jiabao, the former premier of China, see page 92). Some other sites primarily rely on filters that will deny users the ability to post a message if they use a banned word—a practice that Weibo also employs, to a lesser extent.[22] Furthermore, successfully posting a message doesn't necessarily mean it can be read and shared. At times, if a post contains a sensitive word, it might be rendered invisible to others even though you

---

21. Mercifully, yellow has been unblocked since February 2012.

22. For instance, trying to post a message with the word Bloomberg (see page 206) or Wen Jiabao will return this message: 抱歉，此内容违反了《新浪微博社区管理规定 (试行)》或相关法规政策 . . . (Sorry, this content violates "Sina Weibo's Community Guidelines" or related regulations and policies . . .).

can see it on your own timeline.[23] Finally, Weibo's censors can also summarily delete inflammatory messages without any notice.[24] However, the censors are not infallible, and it is possible for posts with banned words to escape the censor's eye—so long as they don't gain too much attention or advocate collective action,[25] or perhaps if they're cleverly embedded inside images or obscured in coded language (see Combining Cyrillic Millions, page 42). Blocking a user's ability to find a term makes it impossible to look for sensitive content, and the censors don't have to delete or filter posts one at a time. Not only is this method more flexible, it's less intrusive. Users might feel outraged if they were faced with an error message when posting their own content, but being unable to find results for a term probably just elicits a shrug. And words that are only temporarily sensitive can be added to the blacklist of search terms one day and removed the next without having had to delete the underlying content.[26] So when censors decide a certain search term is no longer sensitive, as they have done for hundreds

---

23. For instance, for several months in 2012, any post with the word 遊行 (march, see page 135) would cause your post to be disappeared. The Beijing blogger Jason Ng (no relation) documented these vanishing posts and the myriad other ways that Weibo censors in a 2011 post: Jason Ng, "新浪微博给我印象最深刻的10件事," 可能吧 (Kenengba), September 12, 2011, www.kenengba.com/post/3019.html. You can read an English summary at: Steven Millward, "8 Ways That Sina Weibo Will Shut You Up, or Shut You Down," *Tech in Asia*, September 12, 2011, www.techinasia.com/sina -weibo-deleted-banned-blocked.

24. Paul Marks, "Revealed: How China Censors Its Social Networks," *New Scientist*, March 8, 2012, www.newscientist.com/article/dn21553-revealed-how-china-censors -its-social-networks.html.

25. The Gary King article referenced earlier argues that, contrary to popular wisdom, censors allow users to criticize the government online but treat topics that concern potential collective action—demonstrations, protests, petitions, etc.—with widespread deletions, even if the individual post supports the government. The breadth of data collected and new computer-assisted techniques they employ are awe-inspiring, but with regards to this book, their paper concerns only the deletions of posts—not the monitoring of search blocks—and did not encompass Weibo and microblog posts, which they deem to be too short for the content analysis performed with their techniques. Thus, their rigorous conclusions may not be totally applicable to the type of censorship discussed in this book.

26. Charles Custer, "Strange Censorship on Sina Weibo: Bug or Conspiracy?" *Tech in*

of words such as 恋足 (foot fetish; see page 76) and 九一一袭击 (the 9/11 attacks; see page 168) in late January 2012, the switch is flipped and users can suddenly search for foot fetish posts to their hearts' content—so long as they haven't been intimidated by the chilling effects of the previous block.

"Transparency" comes in the form of a notice posted when content is blocked—the same policy promoted by Twitter as a check against censorship.[27] While transparency is generally laudable, it could be argued that these reminders of censorship serve as a form of intimidation, a caution that your Internet activities are being monitored—much as cartoon police figures have been prominently displayed on numerous Chinese websites in recent years.[28] In a way, the search blocks condition users to recognize the limits of acceptable discourse, and even when the limitations are taken away later, the residual effect of the censorship can remain. Such "transparency" serves as an effective training mechanism, thus furthering the goal of decentralizing the censorship and moving the onus for it from the government to the media company and, finally, to the individual.

At the moment, Weibo's search-filtering mechanism is not particularly sophisticated (though post deletions—the so-called soft censorship that takes place behind the scenes without the user ever being aware of it—are relatively more nuanced). The search-filtering mechanism checks the keyword against a blacklist, and if any part of the search term matches any word on the blacklist, the term is blocked. For example, "Nintendo 64" is blocked because "64" is short for June 4, the day of the 1989 Tiananmen crackdown. Thus, any search containing "64" will be blocked, even harmless ones like "Nintendo 64."[29] This is an issue known as the Scunthorpe Problem, so named because the denizens of Scunthorpe, England,

Asia, February 8, 2012, www.penn-olson.com/2012/02/08/strange-censorship-on-sina-weibo-bug-or-conspiracy.

27. "Tweets Still Must Flow," *Twitter Blog*, January 26, 2012, blog.twitter.com/2012/01/tweets-still-must-flow.html.

28. Sami Ben Gharbia, "Chinese Cartoon Cops Patrolling Websites," *Global Voices Advocacy*, August 29, 2007, globalvoicesonline.org/2007/08/29/chinese-cartoon-cops-patrolling-the-web.

29. The number 64 has since been unblocked on Weibo (en.greatfire.org/s.weibo.com

were prevented from signing up for AOL in 1996 because the word "cunt," part of the city's name, was censored.[30]

Over the years, in a series of cat-and-mouse games, Chinese Internet users have developed an extensive series of puns—both visual and homophonous—slang, acronyms, memes, and images to skirt restrictions and censors.[31] Such creative usages may still be helpful in evading the censor's eye on Weibo—using a code makes one's post both less likely to get caught in any automatic search filter, and less likely to be found by a human censor later on. Furthermore, Chinese Internet users have mastered the use of irony as protest, reaching the point where emphatically pro-government comments online such as "Socialism is good"[32] and "I have been represented by my local official"[33] are often meant to be satirical. Filtering tools including the ones Weibo uses in its search engine certainly can't recognize such subtleties. In some respects, the filters are "easy" to defeat, emphasizing just how important those human monitors employed by Weibo are. They have the ability to delete individual posts and even entire accounts, which is what happened to the account of Ai Weiwei, the dissident artist.[34]

* * *

/weibo/64). This is a reminder that to check the latest status of whether a word is still blocked or not, one can reference the list at the end of the book, go to http://s.weibo .com and search for it, or go to GreatFire.org and test there.

30. "Surfing the Net in Bonny Sconny," *Scunthorpe Evening Telegraph*, April 9, 1996. Accessible via David G. Bell, "Computer Underground Digest," ed. Jim Thomas, April 11, 1996, cu-digest.org/CUDS8/cud829.

31. "Glossary," chinaSMACK, accessed December 17, 2012, www.chinasmack.com /glossary.

32. Eric Abrahamsen, "Irony Is Good! How Mao Killed Chinese Humor . . . and How the Internet Is Slowly Bringing It Back Again," *Foreign Policy*, January 12, 2011, www.foreignpolicy.com/articles/2011/01/12/irony_is_good.

33. Anthony Kuhn, "In Changing China, Being 'Suicided' or 'Harmonized,'" *All Things Considered*, NPR, March 19, 2010, www.npr.org/templates/story/story.php ?storyId=124913011.

34. Charles Custer, "Sina Blocks Weibo Accounts in Wake of Ai Weiwei's Fundraising Campaign," *Tech in Asia*, November 7, 2011, www.penn-olson.com/2011/11/07/sina -blocks-weibo-accounts-in-wake-of-ai-weiweis-fundraising-campaign.

Who owns the Internet, and who has the right to control what content is available on it? Is it sovereign territory, or is it free from antiquated earthbound laws? These questions have engaged Internet activists and scholars for over a decade, though to the disappointment of techno-utopians, it turns out that the Internet is very much capable of being regulated, and many governments—even ones in the free Western world who champion free speech and democracy (see Internet monitoring, page 62)—have been perfectly willing to do so.[35] China's "Great Firewall" and "Golden Shield," a vast network of technical controls by which it regulates Internet content, is only the most obvious and extensive. In 2000, Bill Clinton compared censoring the Internet to nailing Jell-O to a wall. But ten years later, China appears to have built an effective harness—self-censorship by companies and netizens (Internet citizens)—to go along with the world's biggest nail gun: tens of thousands of state-employed Internet censors, total government control of overseas Internet data connections, and next-generation monitoring hardware to keep that Jell-O from reaching the floor.

China's ability to censor the Internet extends far beyond being able to flip a "killswitch" as the government did in Xinjiang and turning the Internet off altogether. The way the Chinese government censors the Internet includes technical, behind-the-scenes methods such as bandwidth throttling and keyword filtering, in addition to more overt intervention, including the wholesale blocking of access to websites including Twitter, YouTube, and Facebook.[36] As illustrated by this book, a more subtle method of censorship is to compel Internet companies in China to remove offensive content from their sites and to prevent people from finding and sharing such material in the first place.

---

35. For more about how countries around the world are dealing with issues of Internet regulation, read Rebecca MacKinnon, *Consent of the Networked: The Worldwide Struggle for Internet Freedom* (New York: Basic Books, 2012).

36. For two easy-to-read overviews of the various technical ways China censors the Internet: James Fallows, "'The Connection Has Been Reset,'" *The Atlantic*, March 2008, www.theatlantic.com/magazine/archive/2008/03/-the-connection-has-been -reset/306650; Dinah Gardner, "The Mechanics of China's Internet Censorship," *Uncut, Index on Censorship*, August 9, 2012, uncut.indexoncensorship.org/2012/08 /china-internet-censorship.

Like all major licensed websites in China, Weibo has numerous restrictions on what sort of content it is allowed to host and distribute. In June 2010, China's State Council Information Office released a white paper on Internet usage for the country. Though the paper asserts that Chinese users have the right to freedom of expression online, it also enumerates a prohibition against content that is

> endangering state security, divulging state secrets, subverting state power and jeopardizing national unification; damaging state honor and interests; instigating ethnic hatred or discrimination and jeopardizing ethnic unity; jeopardizing state religious policy, propagating heretical or superstitious ideas; spreading rumors, disrupting social order and stability; disseminating obscenity, pornography, gambling, violence, brutality and terror or abetting crime; humiliating or slandering others, trespassing on the lawful rights and interests of others; and other contents forbidden by laws and administrative regulations.[37]

This is a broad array of off-limit topics, and the fact that a phrase such as "damaging state honor and interests" is not clearly defined is an intentional feature of the Chinese censorship system, a mechanism dubbed by Perry Link "the anaconda in the chandelier"[38]—everyone is aware that it is there, haunting the room, but no one is certain when and why it might strike. Furthermore, Berkeley professor Rachel E. Stern notes that the decentralized nature of the Chinese government means that any number of officials at various levels might take offense at a single controversial post. Thus, there is no single judge of what is allowed or not—instead disparate actors sometimes send out "mixed signals" about what

---

37. "Protecting Internet Security—Govt. White Papers," China.org.cn, accessed December 17, 2012, china.org.cn/government/whitepaper/2010-06/08/content _20207978.htm.

38. Perry Link, "The Anaconda in the Chandelier: Censorship in China Today," US-China Economic and Security Review Commission, originally presented at Woodrow Wilson International Center for Scholars, October 24, 2001, www.uscc.gov/research papers/2000_2003/reports/link.htm.

is acceptable, leaving it up to the content provider to interpret and decide.[39] This vagueness inevitably leads content providers including Sina Weibo to self-censor excessively in order to stay well within the bounds of acceptable discourse. The company and its users may have a sort of sixth sense for knowing what may or may not be off-limits, but the fact that there is no officially published blacklist from the government, coupled with the fear of punishments (including closure of the site), compels them to step even further back from the imaginary line. As Internet scholar Rebecca MacKinnon noted:

> Recent academic research on global Internet censorship has found that in countries where heavy legal liability is imposed on companies, employees tasked with day-to-day censorship jobs have a strong incentive to play it safe and over-censor—even in the case of content whose legality might stand a good chance of holding up in a court of law. Why invite legal hassle when you can just hit "delete"?[40]

Chinese Internet companies are now required to sign the "Public Pledge on Self-Discipline for China Internet Industry," a document with even stricter rules than those listed in the 2010 white paper.[41] So it's no wonder there are companies blocking keywords like "Islam," even though the religion is officially sanctioned under Chinese law.

Chinese government officials send weekly updates to media providers on topics expected to be censored.[42] Otherwise, however, the onus is on the content provider to self-censor, a practice that

39. Rachel E. Stern and Kevin J. O'Brien, "Politics at the Boundary: Mixed Signals and the Chinese State," *Modern China*, September 15, 2011, mcx.sagepub.com /content/early/2011/09/14/0097700411421463.

40. Rebecca MacKinnon, "Stop the Great Firewall of America," *New York Times*, November 15, 2011, www.nytimes.com/2011/11/16/opinion/firewall-law-could -infringe-on-free-speech.html.

41. "Public Pledge on Self-Discipline for China Internet Industry," Hong Kong Human Rights Monitor, accessed December 17, 2012, www.article23.org.hk/english /research/pledgeinternet.RTF.

42. "What Chinese Censors Don't Want You to Know," *New York Times*, March 21, 2010, www.nytimes.com/2010/03/22/world/asia/22banned.html.

Weibo's head editor admitted is "a very big headache,"[43] and during the Southern Weekend censorship controversy (see constitutional court, page 56) even caused one Sina censor to publicly complain, "We were under a lot of pressure. We tried to resist and let the [anti-censorship] messages spread . . . [but] then we got the order from [the Propaganda Department] and we had to delete it. . . . This is a battle."[44] Thus, there are multiple layers of censorship occurring. There is the government-mandated blacklist of off-limit topics[45]— what we'd typically consider censorship—as well as two more subtle forms: the enforced self-censorship by content providers, who must make judgment calls on what needs to be censored in order to stay in the government's good graces; and self-censorship by users, who face the threat of being detained and punished for perceived antigovernment posts (see Internet monitoring, page 62; and Liu Di, page 97). Users are at greater risk than ever now that Weibo and other microblogs request real names in order to register.[46] Though the company and the government claim that this is merely to hold users accountable for spreading misinformation and malicious rumors, it seems clear that such a measure is designed to head off the type of political commentary that could lead to an online-inspired Jasmine Revolution.

China has opened up considerably during its transition from the depths of the Cultural Revolution to where it is today, but vestiges of a level of government control unthinkable in other societies remain prominent features of Chinese life. On the morning of November 8,

43. Elaine Chow, "Quote of the Day: Chen Tong, Head Editor of Sina, on the Annoyance of Censoring Tweets," Shanghaiist, June 14, 2010, shanghaiist.com/2010 /06/14/quote_of_the_day_chen_tong_head_edi.php.

44. Oiwan Lam, "China: Sina Weibo Manager Discloses Internal Censorship Practices," Global Voices Advocacy, January 7, 2013, advocacy.globalvoicesonline .org/2013/01/07/china-sina-weibo-manager-discloses-internal-censorship-practices.

45. These censorship instructions to publishers, broadcasters, and media companies have occasionally been leaked and are cataloged by China Digital Times: "Directives from the Ministry of Truth," China Digital Times, chinadigitaltimes.net/china /directives-from-the-ministry-of-truth.

46. Tania Branigan, "China to Expand Real-Name Registration of Microbloggers," The Guardian, January 18, 2012, www.guardian.co.uk/world/2012/jan/18/china-real -name-registration-microblogging.

2012, less than twenty-four hours after a majority of 125 million Americans voted to give Barack Obama a second term, two thousand delegates of the Chinese Communist Party, along with a number of special attendees, including former head of state Jiang Zemin, filed into Beijing's Great Hall of the People for the CCP's 18th National Congress. They were there to elect[47] the slate of politicians who would be charged with leading China's national government for the next five years; a week later, the political lineups were carefully unveiled to the media as well as to China's 1.3 billion citizens. The process was a piece of highly choreographed and familiar stagecraft, with the new top leader, Xi Jinping, leading his fellow Politburo Standing Committee colleagues onto the stage and China's state television blaring the names of those newly elected in wall-to-wall Party Congress coverage.

However, events leading up to that choreographed "election" were anything but orderly and predictable. The Chinese economy shows signs of slowing down due to continued global financial stress and bad domestic bank loans, with rising inequality causing unrest. China was the villain in a pair of international-headline-grabbing human rights stories in back-to-back years: first for disappearing the notorious Chinese artist Ai Weiwei in 2011, and then for inadvertently letting the blind activist-lawyer Chen Guangcheng escape

---

47. Or "rubber-stamp" if one is a bit more cynical. The delegates who elect the 25-member Politburo do indeed hold elections, but the number of candidates is always the same as the number of positions to be filled, making the process a mere formality. (A delegate can choose to leave the ballot blank for certain individuals as a form of disapproval of that candidate, but this has no bearing on the outcome outside of marring the candidate's ability to claim unanimous approval.) However, some results are left more open to chance. For example, in choosing the 204-member Central Committee, delegates are given more than 204 candidates to select from, and there have been cases of Party favorites who didn't in the end get elected to the Central Committee. But the process certainly isn't democratic: the slate of candidates that the delegates choose from for the Central Committee has been heavily scrutinized beforehand to ensure that only candidates acceptable to the Party are capable of being selected. Trying to guess whether a candidate didn't get elected to the Central Committee because the Party did not put his name up for election on the slate or because he was voted down is a fun parlor game to play with China watchers who follow Beijing politics.

from house arrest to the United States in 2012. Other high-profile controversies included the burial of train cars when survivors were still to be found after the high-speed-rail crash in Wenzhou in July 2011, which in turn was dwarfed by the mother of all scandals in March 2012: the Bo Xilao affair, in which the government official in charge of Chongqing, one of China's largest cities, was sacked due to accusations of corruption, among other improprieties (see page 118).

Throughout it all, Weibo users commented, laughed, and railed against the system, despite the government's and Sina's best efforts to prevent discussion of such matters. As for what this portends for the future, nothing is certain, but the sharing of real-time information in China online—be it through Weibo or through another service, if Weibo is ultimately shut down—is undoubtedly here to stay. The cat-and-mouse game will continue, but Internet users are clever, and with ever-growing information about how companies and governments censor content online, the mice will be harder to catch and silence.

AUTHOR'S NOTE

All the words noted as blocked in this book were indeed blocked on Sina Weibo at some point during 2011–12. However, as the political winds shift and censors update their blacklists of sensitive words, some may have been unblocked and may now be searchable again. For the latest status on whether the word is blocked or not, you can go to s.weibo.com and try searching for it yourself, or go to en.greatfire.org to see a history of when certain words were blocked and unblocked. However, the fact that a word is unblocked from Weibo doesn't mean it's not being censored. The search results that do get returned for the words in this book that have been unblocked may still be heavily censored.

BLOCKED ON WEIBO

1

#government# #CCP# #politics# #nationalism#

江泽民

(**Jiang Zemin** / *Jiāng Zémín*) is a former Chinese politician, who served as China's top government official, general secretary of the Communist Party of China, from 1989 to 2002 and as the head of state, president of the People's Republic of China, from 1993 to 2003.

Why it is blocked: A number of leaders' and politicians' names are banned on Weibo, presumably to prevent insults and virtual paint-splattering.[1] One can view these sorts of social media blocks as a kind of perk of the job, akin to a company car—get to a high-enough position in your field or in the Communist Party and you get rewarded with an online shield against criticism, regardless of whether you are actually a controversial figure or not. Jiang has been officially out of power since 2005, though he still attended National People's Congress meetings up until 2008 and the Party Congress meeting in 2012. He has also been instrumental in the selection of future generations of Party leaders (see Retired Emperor, page 16). After Jiang did not attend the celebration of the ninetieth anniversary of the Communist Party in June 2011, rumors began to circulate that he might be dead. Things reached a peak on July 5 when Weibo decided to try and quash the rumors by censoring all searches with the character 江, which is the Chinese word for river as well as Jiang's surname (see obituary, page 117).[2] As you can

---

1. In February 2006, a Chinese journalist was freed after spending nearly seventeen years in prison for splattering paint on a portrait of Mao during the 1989 prodemocracy protests in Tiananmen Square. Jim Yardley, "Man Freed After Years in Jail for Mao Insult," *New York Times*, February 23, 2006, www.nytimes.com/2006/02/23 /international/asia/23beijing.html.
2. Sophie Beach, "Rumors of Jiang Zemin's Death Circulate Online; Censors Respond (Updated)," *China Digital Times*, July 6, 2011, chinadigitaltimes.net/2011/07 /rumors-of-jiang-zemins-death-circulate-online-censors-respond.

imagine, blocking searches for all posts with the word "river" was probably a bit much, and bloggers had a field day laughing at the overvigilant censors. The rumors weren't dispelled for good until Jiang appeared in public in October 2011, by which time one could search for rivers again.

元老

(**veteran** or **an old leader** / *yuánlǎo*) In the context of the Chinese Communist Party this term refers to the **Eight Elders**, also sarcastically called "the Eight Immortals." These former senior leaders, headed by Deng Xiaoping, held substantial power during the 1980s and 1990s even after they had retired.

Why it is blocked: Though the Eight Elders were not the heads of state and were not recognized as an official body in the constitution, major decisions still had to be run past them even after they had retired from public office. During the June 4, 1989, student demonstrations in Tiananmen Square, the Elders were consulted throughout, and it was only with their approval that the top leaders legitimately in office agreed to send in the troops to quell the protests. A new wave of elders (including Jiang Zemin) has since replaced the original eight, but these current elders do not wield the power that the body did during the 1980s and 1990s (see Retired Emperor, page 16).

中联办

(**Liaison Office** / *Zhōngliánbàn*) is short for **the Liaison Office of the Central People's Government in the Hong Kong Special Administrative Region**, an organ of the PRC[3] government tasked with coordinating economic, cultural, educational, and technological exchanges between Hong Kong and mainland China. Formed in May 1947, it was named the Xinhua News Agency Hong Kong Branch[4] before the 1997 handover of Hong Kong.

Why it is blocked: Both the agency's current and previous names belie its full mission: it's not just a run-of-the-mill press office or lovey-dovey cultural exchange program, but rather is charged with a more active propaganda and political administration role, including promoting pro-PRC relations and collaborating with local departments in overseeing military forces in Hong Kong. The first post-handover director of the agency, Jiang Enzhu, declared that the Liaison Office would curtail its reach and promised political noninterference in Hong Kong, but Hong Kong residents remained highly skeptical, even more so after Cao Erbao, head of research at

---

3. PRC is short for People's Republic of China, the formal name for China. Taiwan's formal name is Republic of China, often shortened as ROC. Since England handed over Hong Kong in 1997 and Portugal handed over Macao in 1999, both Hong Kong and Macao have been governed by the PRC, but since they are afforded special laws that allow them greater autonomy—they have their own quasi-independent governments, and their media is much freer than that of the PRC—they are not often included when referring to "mainland" China and, depending on the context, may or may not be included when referring to the PRC.
4. Xinhua is China's dominant news agency, sort of like America's Associated Press, with reporters around the world. However, it is also an official body and accountable to China's State Council—as if the AP's CEO were somehow appointed by the White House.

the agency, wrote in a 2008 article that Hong Kong was and should be jointly governed by the local and mainland governments—a direct contradiction of the "one country, two systems" policy (see Article 23, page 24).[5] Numerous protests have taken place in front of the Liaison Office in past years, and even the comings and goings of local politicians to and from the agency's Hong Kong offices are closely watched.[6]

---

5. Cao Erbao, "Governing Hong Kong Under the Conditions of 'One Country, Two Systems,'" translated by Margaret Ng, Civic Party, accessed December 16, 2012, www.civicparty.hk/cp/media/pdf/090506_cao_eng.pdf. Original Chinese article published as "「一國兩制」 條件下香港的管治力量," 學習時報 (Study Times), January 29, 2008.

6. Gary Cheung, Tanna Chong, and Peter So, "Riddle of Liaison Office Visits," *South China Morning Post*, December 15, 2011, www.scmp.com/article/987790/riddle-liaison-office-visits.

政变

(**coup d'état** / *zhèngbiàn*) is a sudden, illegal overthrow of a government.

Why it is blocked: This search ban was noticed on Twitter as early as Tuesday, March 20, 2012, 8:13 P.M. Beijing time[7] (though inklings of potential censorship were hinted at as early as the previous night[8]). The ban was in reaction to the wild rumors that a coup was taking place in Beijing at the time, with the military intervening on Bo Xilai's behalf (see page 118) to arrest Hu Jintao and Wen Jiabao. Ultimately, the rumors were just that, rumors. The *Los Angeles Times* noted that Beijing had ordered 3,300 party cadres home for "ideological retraining" (that is, classes on how to be a proper Communist leader), thus perhaps explaining the heightened military presence in Beijing during those days.[9] Chinese history is no stranger to coups; examples include the 1927 Communist purge by Chiang Kai-shek and the end to the Hundred Days' Reform in 1898.

7. Bill Bishop, "'政变'(Coup) Is Now a Banned Search Term on Sina Weibo 根据相关法律法规和政策, '政变' 搜索结果未予显示," Twitter, March 20, 2012, twitter.com/#!/niubi/status/182077522043875329.

8. Adam Minter, "Chinese Coup Rumors Run Wild Online, Then Disappear," *Bloomberg*, March 21, 2012, www.bloomberg.com/news/2012-03-21/chinese-coup -rumors-run-wild-online-then-disappear-adam-minter.html.

9. Barbara Demick, "China Coup Rumors May Be Wild, but Tension Is Real," *Los Angeles Times*, March 22, 2012, articles.latimes.com/2012/mar/22/world/la-fg-china -coup-rumors-20120323.

上海帮

(Shanghai Gang or **Shanghai Clique** / *Shànghǎi bāng*) is a nickname given to a group of high-level Communist Party politicians who were most prominent during the 1990s and early 2000s. These politicians usually had strong ties to then president Jiang Zemin, who came to power as the mayor and party chief in Shanghai. Jiang packed the Politburo with his former Shanghai subordinates, but since he left office in 2003, the Shanghai Gang's influence has arguably waned,[10] though Jiang remains very powerful (see Retired Emperor, page 16).

Why it is blocked: 上海帮, like "Shanghai Gang" in English, has a decidedly pejorative connotation, implying underhanded dealings and cronyism. Richard McGregor's *The Party* has an excellent chapter on how the central government was able to rein in the group's power by arresting and imprisoning one of Jiang's most trusted allies, Chen Liangyu, on corruption charges.[11] Since the Communist Party essentially runs China, it can be helpful to think of informal subgroups within the Chinese Communist Party (CCP) such as the Shanghai Gang and the Youth League faction[12] (团派 / *tuánpài*—also blocked on Weibo) as China's de facto political par-

---

10. Cheng Li, "Was the Shanghai Gang Shanghaied? The Fall of Chen Liangyu and the Survival of Jiang Zemin's Faction," *China Leadership Monitor*, Hoover Institution, February 28, 2007, www.hoover.org/publications/china-leadership -monitor/article/5877.

11. Richard McGregor, *The Party: The Secret World of China's Communist Rulers* (New York: HarperPerennial, 2012), 135–69.

12. Hu Jintao's so-called political party, since he rose up through the Communist Youth League, an organization that serves as a training ground for future Communist Party members.

ties, though with less-clear distinctions in terms of who belongs to what.[13] These alliances are often based on personal connections as well as ideology. In a country whose government presents itself as unified on all fronts, writing about such political infighting is no doubt frowned upon.

13. As examples, Xi Jinping was a former Youth League member but is also considered to be a protégé of Jiang Zemin, rising to heir apparent in 2007 with Jiang's heavy backing over Hu Jintao's preferred candidate, Li Keqiang. Another example is Li Yuanchao, Politburo member and former head of the influential Organization Department, which is in charge of vetting future Communist leaders and appointees. Though Li was born in Shanghai and his father was a major Shanghai political figure, he isn't associated with the Shanghai faction, and if anything, he's more aligned with the Youth League, as he has supported Hu's policies over the years and was himself a Youth League member. Since his father was an important Communist politician, Li is also considered to be part of the Crown Prince Party (see page 18), another loose collective that includes people ranging from Bo Xilai to Xi Jinping.

黄雀行动

(**Operation Yellowbird** / *Huángquè Xíngdòng*) was a Hong Kong–based effort initiated after the June 4, 1989, crackdown on Tiananmen Square to assist Chinese political dissidents in leaving the mainland. From 1989 to 1997, a group of Hong Kong activists, international diplomats, businessmen, and celebrities worked with Hong Kong crime bosses and smugglers to guide more than four hundred dissidents out of China. The program has been called the Chinese Underground Railroad.

Why it is blocked: Not only does the operation deal with politically sensitive people—June 4 student leaders Wu'er Kaixi, Chai Ling, and others left the country with Yellowbird's assistance—but it also touches on sovereignty issues, as well as the obvious rifts in the Hong Kong–China relationship. Foreign nations and diplomats actively bent laws to allow dissidents to sneak into Hong Kong and then find safe passage out to countries including the United States and France. Though China fiercely objected to such interference, *The Independent* conjectured that China might have had cause for letting dissidents slip through its fingers: "Apart from the connivance of sympathetic Chinese officials, Yellowbird's high rate of success appears to owe something to inertia in the government, which can find it more convenient to let dissidents leave the country than have them remain to cause trouble."[14] Whether it was a convenient solution or not, Operation Yellowbird highlights just how

---

14. Stephen Vines, "Time for the Yellow Bird of Hong Kong to Fly. Exclusive: Activists Who Helped Chinese Political Fugitives Are Planning Their Own Escape," *The Independent*, May 11, 1997, www.independent.co.uk/news/world/time-for-the -yellow-bird-of-hong-kong-to-fly-1260886.html.

differently Hong Kong and China viewed the June 4 incident, a touchy topic that mainland Chinese leaders will have to confront in the coming years as China continues to try and integrate Hong Kong politically, socially, and economically.

抵制日货
抵制家乐福

(**Boycott Japanese goods** / *dǐzhì Rìhuò*) and 抵制家乐福 (**Boycott Carrefour** / *dǐzhì Jiālèfú*) were two separate grassroots movements in recent years aimed at demonstrating Chinese anger at Japan and the French retailer Carrefour, respectively. Though they took place in different years[15] and for different reasons,[16] both were inspired by patriotic, verging on ultranationalist, sentiment that played up China's role as a country that has been victimized in the past but would no longer be bullied. (See medicine patch flag, page 194, for more about anti-Japan sentiment in China.)

Why it is blocked: For each event, anger was expressed virtually as well as with demonstrations and a call to boycott goods. In each case, the central government either appeared to support tacitly initial protests or made no strong efforts to tamp them

---

15. Japan boycotts took place in 2005, 2010, and 2012, among others; the Carrefour boycott was in 2008.

16. Japan for continuing resentment over atrocities and the occupation of parts of China during the Sino-Japanese War, the cleansing of negative World War II–era Japanese acts from textbooks in 2005, former Japanese prime minister Junichiro Koizumi's annual visits to the Yasukuni Shrine, and disputes over islands in the East China Sea, among others; Carrefour because in the run-up to the 2008 Olympics in Beijing, the Olympic torch relay was interrupted several times across the world by human rights protesters, most notoriously in France when the Chinese Paralympic fencer Jin Jing was tackled in her wheelchair while carrying the torch, and Carrefour, whose supermarkets are common in Chinese cities and allegedly also donated to Free Tibet causes, served as a convenient scapegoat.

down, but as demonstrations grew out of control in each instance, the authorities reacted by reining in the outrage. The existence of a block on 抵制日货 on Weibo seems to be a legacy of these previous demonstrations and is not new. In fact, in the midst of the most recent wave of anti-Japan protests over the contested Diaoyu Islands in September 2012, the term was unblocked, indicating a potential shift—or perhaps, merely a short-term tactical decision.

太上皇

(**Emperor Emeritus** or **Retired Emperor** / *tàishàng huáng*) is a title occasionally given to fathers who have abdicated the throne to their sons. The honorific was used most commonly in China, but was also used in Japan, Korea, and Vietnam. In China today, 太上皇 has also come to mean "**backstage ruler**," that is, someone who has officially stepped down from office but who continues to wield considerable influence on the current leaders. The best example today is Jiang Zemin, who allegedly dictated many personnel changes during the Hu Jintao administration. Jiang's influence on Hu was greatest in the years immediately after Jiang retired in 2003, though he continued to hold the top military post until 2005. A number of his protégés, known as the Shanghai Gang (see page 10), held positions in the Politburo and the State Council, China's main decision-making and administrative bodies, as well as other powerful positions. However, his influence was deeply undercut in 2006 when Hu forced out Shanghai mayor Chen Liangyu, a close Jiang ally, on corruption charges. Even so, Jiang was not sidelined completely: rumors swirled that Ling Jihua's demotion—he had served as Hu's so-called chief of staff and was seen as a shoo-in for promotion to the Politburo—in September 2012 after his son was connected to a scandalous Ferrari accident was likely orchestrated by Jiang.[17]

Why it is blocked: The term has been used to disparage the con-

---

17. "儿子车祸丑闻令计划晋升受阻," BBC China Online, September 3, 2012, www .bbc.co.uk/zhongwen/simp/chinese_news/2012/09/120903_ling_jihua_sandal _politics.shtml. Xi Jinping's elevation to general secretary over Hu's preferred candidate, Li Keqiang, is also seen as evidence of Jiang's continued political relevance at the expense of the leadership nominally in power (see Shanghai Gang, page 11, note 13).

temporary Chinese political system and its lack of transparency. The implication is not only that the Chinese political system is not representative, but that the supposed representatives aren't even actually in power and are in fact controlled by a separate puppet master (see Zhao Ziyang's *Prisoner of State* for a firsthand look at how top leaders needed to arrange secret meetings with Deng Xiaoping[18] totally apart from their "regular" private meetings with the Politburo in order to maneuver the group into ordering the crackdown on Tiananmen Square in 1989).

18. Though Deng never held the top position in the Chinese government or in the Communist Party—in fact, his highest-ranked title was chairman of the National Committee of the CPPCC (Chinese People's Consultative Conference), which is fifth in the current order of precedence in the Chinese government—he was widely acknowledged as the "paramount ruler" of China and was head of China's Central Advisory Commission, a group that had great overlap with the Eight Elders (see page 6).

太子党

(literally, **Crown Prince Party** or **princelings** / *tàizǐ dǎng*) is a derogatory term for the children and grandchildren of major leaders of the Communist Party, the implication being that these privileged members are exploiting their fathers' and grandfathers' names and connections (the so-called *guanxi*) for economic and political advantage.

Why it is blocked: For a party that prides itself on personal discretion, a number of scandals have involved the obscene amounts of wealth that political leaders and their children have amassed, despite the moderate salaries that cadres officially take home. Wen Yunsong (see page 92), son of current premier Wen Jiabao, and Bo Xilai (see page 118), son of Bo Yibo, one of the Eight Elders (see page 6), are just two examples of this phenomenon. Bo Xilai's son, also an involuntary "member" of the Crown Prince Party, was himself involved in two separate scandals: one when online commenters dug up pictures of him partying, and a second when rumors flew that he had picked up U.S. ambassador Jon Huntsman's daughter for a dinner date in a red Ferrari.[19] Another princeling, Ling Gu, the twenty-three-year-old son of Hu Jintao's then chief of staff Ling Jihua, also was embroiled in controversy over a sports car. In March 2012, Ling Gu crashed his Ferrari, killing himself and injuring his two female passengers. Though rumors and photos of the grisly accident initially circulated on Weibo, a cover-up hid

---

19. This story was eventually disproved. It was not in fact a red Ferrari, but rather a much more modest black Audi sedan—albeit chauffeured by Bo's personal driver. David Barboza and Edward Wong, "Details Are Refuted in Tale of Bo Guagua's Red Ferrari," *New York Times*, April 30, 2012, www.nytimes.com/2012/05/01/world/asia/in-china-details-in-bo-guagua-episode-challenged.html.

his true identity until it was confirmed in September that it was indeed Ling Jihua's son. Ling was demoted at roughly the same time, and his name (令计划) was blocked at various points during the following months.

新左派

(**the New Left** / *xīn zuŏpài*), in its Western usage, refers to a collection of ideas and people from the 1960s that rejected the traditional Left and its emphasis on labor and class struggles. Instead, those in the New Left called for new approaches to Marxism that departed from orthodox theory and instead focused on student activism or other alternative "anti-Establishment" movements. The "Chinese New Left," in contrast, is a term which arose in the 1990s and was used by critics on the Chinese Right (free-market, pro–individual rights, anti-Maoist, "liberal")[20] to denigrate those who argued against the incorporation of capitalist principles into the Chinese economy, in an attempt to smear them as Maoists. Since the current Chinese economic model is a mixture of neoliberalism and socialism, the Chinese New Left can seem at times conservative (and supportive of the Communist Party) as well as critical of

---

20. In China the Left is considered "conservative" and believes in, on the whole, more socialist, nationalist, and Maoist principles than the Right. When trying to reconcile this seeming disconnect with American political terminology, it is perhaps helpful to link the Left with a more pro-state (strong-government) stance and the Right with an individual-rights (small-government) position. It just so happens that in China the Left is the more "conservative" tendency (trying to maintain the traditions of Mao and Communism) while the Right, which takes many of its influences from the West, is the new "liberal" strain that seeks to reform the Chinese government and economy. In (radically simplified) Chinese terms, anti-Japanese sentiment and the New Deal would be placed on the Left, the Tiananmen Square protests and privatizing state industries on the Right. For more clarification, see Tea Leaf Nation's translation of a chart detailing the two sides: Tea Leaf Nation, "A Pictorial Guide to China's Politics: Left v. Right," February 29, 2012, tealeafnation.com/2012/02/a-pictorial-guide-to -chinas-politics-left-v-right.

the government (when attacking the government's neoliberal approach to the economy).[21]

Why it is blocked: Though the Chinese New Left was shaped in the 1990s by a number of intellectuals, economists, and writers (many of whom, including the scholar and leading New Left figure Wang Hui, are reluctant to embrace the term)[22] with nuanced positions on free speech, democracy, global trade, environmental protection, and the Cultural Revolution, today the New Left is popularly associated with Mao revivalism and anticapitalist movements, a mixture that alarms many leaders who remember the pernicious excesses of the Cultural Revolution and its wave of uncontrollable popular attacks on innocent landowners and businesses, among others. Bo Xilai (see page 118) was in many ways the face of this so-called New Left: while he was party secretary in Chongqing he mandated the singing of Revolutionary-era songs, transmitted quotes from Mao's *Little Red Book* by text message to everyone in Chongqing, and erected statues of Mao throughout the city, in addition to reorienting the city's economy around state-owned industries. Bo was ousted from office in April 2012, but 新左派 had been blocked well before then.

21. For an excellent discussion of the current state of China's intellectual sphere and the development of the New Left, listen to Kaiser Kuo and Jeremy Goldkorn's podcast with guest Mark Leonard: Sinica, "China 3.0," Popup Chinese, December 14, 2012, popupchinese.com/lessons/sinica/china-30.

22. "Wang was quick to say that he disliked the New Left label, even though he has used it himself. He prefers the term 'critical intellectual' for himself and like-minded colleagues, some of whom are also part of China's nascent activist movement in the countryside, working to alleviate rural poverty and environmental damage." Pankaj Mishra, "China's New Left Calls for a Social Alternative," *New York Times*, October 13, 2006, www.nytimes.com/2006/10/13/world/asia/13iht-left.3148238.html?page wanted=all.

西乌旗

(**West Ujimqin** / Xī Wūqí) in Chinese is 西乌珠穆沁旗, but it is abbreviated as 西乌旗. West Ujimqin is a "banner" or county in Inner Mongolia. Inner Mongolia is one of five autonomous province-level regions in China,[23] and like the other autonomous regions, it has a substantial minority population, with 17 percent of its 24 million people being ethnically Mongolian.

Why it is blocked: On May 10, 2011, a Mongol herdsman was struck and killed by an ethnic Han truck driver while he was attempting to block coal-mining trucks from intruding on private grazing lands. The hit-and-run death reignited long-standing resentment of outside companies who have exploited Inner Mongolia's vast mineral resources and damaged the land. Gruesome photos of the man's bloodied body were circulated online, and demonstrations throughout Xilingol (the prefecture that contains West Ujimqin) began two weeks after the man's death. Protesters—including several hundred herders in West Ujimqin and two thousand high school students in Xilinhot—marched on government offices, and the central government quickly dispatched riot police to quell the demonstrations. Protests continued for another week, spreading to the region's cap-

---

23. The other four are Xinjiang, Tibet, Ningxia, and Guangxi. These four, along with Inner Mongolia, technically have more legislative rights and discretion in economic policy planning than other Chinese provinces but, overall, don't differ too much. Hong Kong and Macao are not autonomous regions, but are rather special administrative regions (SARs—not to be confused with the flulike disease SARS, severe acute respiratory syndrome). SARs are also province-level administrative districts but have much greater independence than autonomous regions do. SARs are not to be confused with SEZs (special economic zones), which are other specially designated cities and regions where national economic and government restrictions were relaxed, encouraging free-market-oriented reforms and more foreign investment.

ital, Hohhot. The driver of the truck was sentenced to death on June 8 and speedily executed on August 18.

Though ethnic clashes in Tibet and Xinjiang have been widely publicized, strife in Inner Mongolia has mostly flown under the radar because, unlike in Tibet and Xinjiang, protests in Inner Mongolia are typically not related to issues of autonomy or the legitimacy of the Communist Party leaders in the region.[24] In fact, Enghebatu Togochog, director of the Southern Mongolian Human Rights Information Center, a New York–based advocacy group for Inner Mongolian human rights, noted that in the 2011 protests, "people demanded legal rights for Mongolians, for herders. They didn't mention higher autonomy or independence. Their goals are practical, so the government can't find an excuse to crack down hard on them."[25] However, economic inequality and ecological destruction have become major issues for native Inner Mongolians, and so even though ethnic tensions may be low compared to Xinjiang or Tibet, there is potential for more future conflict.[26]

24. Wu Zhong, "Green Motives in Inner Mongolian Unrest," *Asia Times*, June 8, 2011, www.atimes.com/atimes/China/MF08Ad01.html.

25. Jaime FlorCruz, "Inner Mongolia Beset by Ethnic Conflict," CNN, June 2, 2011, articles.cnn.com/2011-06-02/world/inner.mongolia.unrest_1_mongolians-mining-nicholas-bequelin?_s=PM:WORLD.

26. Though 西乌旗 is blocked, its full name and other place-names involved in the demonstrations are unblocked.

二十三条

(**Article 23** / *ershisān tiáo*) is a reference to a provision in the Basic Law of the Hong Kong Special Administrative Region of the People's Republic of China (香港特別行政區基本法第二十三條). The Basic Law serves as Hong Kong's constitution. It was drafted by a committee of members from Hong Kong and mainland China, and its principles are in accordance with the "one country, two systems" principle (see Liaison Office, page 7) that China had agreed to with the United Kingdom. The Basic Law was adopted in 1990 and took effect in 1997 once the United Kingdom handed Hong Kong over to China. Article 23 of the Basic Law states: "The Hong Kong Special Administrative Region shall enact laws on its own to prohibit any act of treason, secession, sedition, subversion against the Central People's Government. . . ."

Why it is blocked: Article 23 gives the Hong Kong government wide-ranging latitude to pass any number of security laws if it chooses to do so, including ones that would infringe on freedom of speech, the press, and assembly, but Chinese and Hong Kong officials rightfully judged that doing so at the time of the law's adoption in 1997 would be met with great public resistance. However, in 2002, PRC officials figured that in the post-9/11 climate, with the United States successfully passing its own Patriot Act, the timing was right to push Hong Kong officials to pass security legislation based on Article 23. On February 26, 2003, a security bill was submitted to the Hong Kong legislative council, but after five hundred thousand people protested against the bill during the annual July 1 march from Victoria Park (see page 50), key supporters of the bill withdrew their support, and the bill was shelved on September 5. References to Article 23 still rankle Hong Kong citizens who are wary of the Chinese government meddling in their affairs. Since the issue of passing an Article 23–based security law is so contentious and capable of arousing the anger of so many Hong Kong citizens, it appears the term has become sensitive, despite the fact that authorities support it. This is a good example of when the blocked term isn't considered "bad" by the government; the purpose of censoring it is simply to prevent controversy and discussion.

二月逆流

(**February Countercurrent** / *Eryuè Nìliú*) was the purging of a number of "counterrevolutionary" military leaders who spoke out against the Cultural Revolution in February of 1967.

Why it is blocked: The Cultural Revolution began the previous year when Mao Zedong led a drive to expel a number of disloyal officials, eventually gaining full control of the press and military. Like student groups (known as the Red Guard) who demonstrated against their elders, teachers, and intellectuals, government officials also took their cues from Mao and accused their political rivals of being anti-Revolutionary, forcing them from office and into reeducation camps. Soon, internal power struggles became a game of who could preemptively accuse the other of being anti-Revolutionary.

In February of 1967, the political cleansing was extended to the military. A number of prominent generals who had fought during the Chinese civil war and helped establish the People's Republic of China finally came out against this new wave of purges and called the Cultural Revolution a mistake. Unfortunately, even their seemingly rock-solid Revolutionary credentials were not enough to protect them, and they were denounced as the "February Countercurrent." The generals were expelled, and the national army lost power to myriad Red Guard groups. The government and Beijing fell into chaos, and it wasn't until the 1970s that things were fully stabilized. Though Mao is still hailed today by the Communist Party, Deng Xiaoping acknowledged in 1981 that Mao's actions were 70 percent positive and 30 percent negative. The excesses of the Cultural Revolution are still officially blamed on Mao's wife, Jiang Qing, and three of her confederates, the so-called Gang of Four, but Mao's approval of many of their actions continues to make reappraisal of that period sensitive.

宪政民主

(**constitutional democracy** / *xiànzhèng mínzhǔ*), also known as liberal democracy, is generally classified as a government that holds free elections and has a separation of powers between different branches of government, among other principles.

Why it is blocked: Today, China is not a constitutional democracy, though it has attempted to initiate certain reforms in recent years to perhaps move it in that direction—if future party leaders so choose.[27] Direct elections take place at certain local levels, and the country's Supreme Court appeared to be moving toward becoming an autonomous body during the 2000s before its power was curtailed (see constitutional court, page 56). However, on the whole, any discussion of political reform is strictly suppressed (see charter, page 141). For instance, when Premier Wen Jiabao made references in a number of 2010 speeches to China's need to take up more democratic measures,[28] his remarks were censored by state media.[29]

27. Chrystia Freeland of Reuters writes that countries like China and Russia have cleverly exploited their spoken desire for greater freedoms in order to justify their current more illiberal practices—essentially, declaring that they are on the right path, but just need more time. Chrystia Freeland, "Russia and China, Challenges for Liberal Democracy," *New York Times*, June 28, 2012, www.nytimes.com/2012/06/29 /world/europe/29iht-letter29.html?pagewanted=all.
28. Tania Branigan, "Wen Jiabao Talks of Democracy and Freedom in CNN Interview," *The Guardian*, October 4, 2010, www.guardian.co.uk/world/2010/oct/04 /wen-jiabao-china-reform-cnn-interview.
29. Malcolm Moore, "Chinese Prime Minister Censored by Communist Party," *The Telegraph*, October 13, 2010, www.telegraph.co.uk/news/worldnews/asia/china /8060819/Chinese-prime-minister-censored-by-Communist-party.html.

民族问题

(**minority problem** / *mínzú wèntí*) refers to the issues the Chinese government and ethnic minorities face in a country that is over 90 percent Han, the dominant ethnic group in China. In September 2009, President Hu Jintao called on state officials to do a better job of relating to and understanding their minority constituents, calling ethnic unity one of the keys to social harmony.

Why it is blocked: Though China has officially recognized fifty-six native ethnic groups, all of which have an array of unique concerns and issues, the two most "problematic" for state officials are the Uyghurs in Xinjiang (see Kashi, page 172) and the Tibetans in Tibet (see Tibetan protest, page 181), regions where unrest has broken out in recent years. A mix of ethnic tensions, desires for independence or greater autonomy, and increasing income inequality make these particularly volatile regions, especially as more Han Chinese migrate to Xinjiang and Tibet. Government officials have responded by investing heavily in the regions' infrastructures and social welfare systems in a sort of effort to buy peace and acquiescence in these border provinces.

Africans in Guangzhou, Guangdong, also made headlines when they protested against police violence and harassment in June 2012, after an African man died in police custody, another example of a minority "problem" that China will face as its majority Han citizens learn to handle immigrants who now see China as an attractive destination.[30]

---

30. For a discussion with Evan Osnos about Africans in Guangzhou: Sinica, "The One Child Policy," Popup Chinese, June 22, 2012, popupchinese.com/lessons/sinica/the -one-child-policy. See also Gordon Mathews's fascinating *Ghetto at the Center of the World: Chungking Mansions, Hong Kong* (Chicago: University of Chicago Press, 2011).

红色恐怖

(**red terror** / *hóngsè kǒngbù*) can refer to any number of violent campaigns of suppression, through mass arrests and executions, of suspected enemy forces. Among them are that carried out by the Soviet Russian Bolsheviks in 1918, the last six weeks of the "Reign of Terror" during the French Revolution in 1794, the campaign by the Spanish Republicans during the Spanish civil war in the 1930s, and the social upheaval during the Cultural Revolution in China.

Why it is blocked: In China, the red terror began in 1966 and ended with the Gang of Four's arrest in 1976 (see February Countercurrent, page 26). It was red not only for the bloodshed, but also because most of the violence was carried out by Communist youth groups known as the Red Guard (red being the representative color of Communism). Millions died due to the violence and instability caused by the Cultural Revolution, and the government has been loath to admit to past mistakes, fearing that discussing the past could arouse long-suppressed anger among the victims, most of whose tormentors have never been brought to justice.

雪山狮子旗

(**snow lion flag** / *xuěshān shīzi qí*) is the state and military flag of Tibet. It has six red bands representing the six original ancestors of Tibet, a rising sun over a mountain, the three-colored jewel of the Buddha, and a pair of snow lions, Tibet's national emblem. Though it was the official flag of Tibet, it was rarely used before 1959, when China took control of the region.

Why it is blocked: After the failed Tibetan rebellion of 1959, the Dalai Lama went into exile. The snow lion flag soon came to represent the Tibetan independence movement and is now a well-known symbol of the Free Tibet movement. The flag is no longer recognized by China, as it is considered an affront to its sovereignty over Tibet.

新西山会议

(New Western Hills Symposium / *Xīn Xīshān huìyì*) was a secret conference of intellectuals and policy makers that met on March 4, 2006, to discuss market reforms to China's economic system. It was held in China's scenic Western Hills, thirty miles west of Beijing's center. The Western Hills are also the site of China's military head-quarters[31] and home to a number of famous Buddhist temples.

Why it is blocked: The meeting was organized by Gao Shangquan, the director of the government-affiliated Research Society for the Reform of China's Economic System, in the midst of an apparent backlash against China's decades-long embrace of capitalism. In March 2005, one of China's leading economists and pro-market advocates, Liu Guoguang, surprised many by advocating the need for a proper balance between socialism and capitalism. Later in August, another prominent academic, Gong Xintian, came out against a new property law (see violent demolition, page 179) that was under consideration in the National People's Congress, criticizing the drafters as slaves to neoliberalism and not offering equal protections to all citizens. All of this followed controversy set off by economist Lang Xianping's criticism of government corruption on his popular TV talk show. With public opinion seemingly turning against China's neoliberal reforms, market reformers met to discuss ways to prevent dissent.

However, a transcript of the meeting was leaked online and conservative scholars and netizens, what some have called China's New Left (see page 20), claimed that the inflammatory rhetoric and proposals revealed in the transcript were evidence of a vast

---

31. "China's Military Center Off-Limits," *Washington Times*, October 14, 2005, www.washingtontimes.com/news/2005/oct/14/20051014-114525-9990r.

conspiracy to overtake the Chinese government with a neoliberal ideology. The Maoist website *Utopia* organized much of this online criticism, but the government quickly stepped in to head off any challenges to China's path toward capitalism. On March 6, 2006, Hu Jintao addressed the Shanghai National People's Congress: "The bottom line of furthering socialist modernization at the new historical starting point is to deepen reform and expand opening up."[32] Apparently, Weibo has decided to toe the government line by blocking searches for the New Western Hills Symposium and the discussions of a neoliberal takeover of the government.

---

32. For more, read Yuezhi Zhao's "Challenging Neoliberalism?" in *Communication in China: Political Economy, Power, and Conflict* (Lanham, MD: Rowman & Littlefield, 2008), 287–331.

中国泛蓝联盟

(the Union of Chinese Nationalists / *Zhōngguó Fànlán Liánméng*), also known as the Pan-Blue Alliance of Chinese Nationalists,[33] is an unrecognized political party in China that is anti-Communist, opposes Taiwanese independence, and supports a Chinese transition toward liberal democracy (see page 27).

Why it is blocked: Though the Chinese government does sanction a number of non-Communist political parties in the name of diversity, these groups are without actual power (see Communist dog, page 198, note 12, and Lei Jieqiong, page 107). Those not sanctioned—and thus not regulated by the government—are deemed illegal and prone to suppression due to fears that they may present a genuine challenge to Communist rule. In 2007, China's Taiwan Affairs Office declared the UOCN "unregistered and illegal."[31] Being anti-Communist and supporting political reform efforts are nonstarters for any collective group in China, let alone a political party, so it is inevitable that the UOCN would be suppressed in mainland China.

---

33. Not to be confused with the Taiwanese group the Pan-Blue Coalition, which is opposed in Taiwan by the minority Pan-Green Coalition. The Pan-Blues were once more actively pro-reunification with the mainland, while the Pan-Greens were stridently pro-independence, but each side has since moderated its position in the past decade. Today, the Pan-Blue is in power and advocates greater economic linkages with mainland China, but prefers to maintain the current status quo politically.
34. "国台办: 大陆泛蓝联盟属非法组织 与国民党无关," 黄河新闻网 (Yellow River News), *People's Daily*, April 25, 2007, www.sxgov.cn/xwjj/443732.shtml.

2

#dissent# #censorship# #justice#

五毛

(literally, **fifty cents** / *wǔmáo*), short for 五毛党 (*Wǔmáo Dǎng*) or **50 Cent Party**, is a pejorative term for Internet commentators (see page 61) hired by the Chinese government to post online comments favorable to the Communist Party and China.[1] They can be sent on the offensive or defensive—that is, they will often rush in to assert their approval of controversial government measures or swarm to criticize stories and posts, including those in English, that put China in a bad light. They get their name from the supposed fifty cents they earn from each post (五 means five and 毛 means dime; fifty Chinese cents is roughly equivalent to eight American cents). In 2005, school officials at Nanjing University hired students to locate anti-Party or anti-China content online and to respond in the comments, one of the first known cases of 五毛–type behavior; the national government began its own program at roughly the same time.

Why it is blocked: Though there has already been much media coverage of China's professional web commentators, and the government has implicitly acknowledged their presence and importance,[2] it still does no good (from the Communist Party's perspective, that is) to have accusations of 五毛 every time someone makes a pro-China comment.

---

1. Many more are volunteers who post pro-China comments out of a sense of patriotic duty.

2. David Bandurski, "Propaganda Leaders Scurry Off to Carry Out the 'Spirit' of Hu Jintao's 'Important' Media Speech," China Media Project, June 25, 2008, cmp.hku.hk /2008/06/25/1079.

四君子

(**the Four Gentlemen** / *sì jūnzi*) refers to four plants: the orchid, the bamboo, the chrysanthemum, and the plum blossom. 君子 is a Confucian concept that is roughly translated into English as "gentlemen" but which actually encompasses an entire virtuous way of living as espoused in Confucius's teachings. The four flowers are commonly depicted in traditional Chinese paintings.

Why it is blocked: There are two differing explanations. From Twitter user abingor: "四君子 refers to the four arrested villagers during the Protests of Wukan."[3] An anonymous Tumblr user provides an alternative explanation: "For me it's obvious why it's blocked, because it refers to them: 刘晓波, 周舵, 高新, 和侯德健[4] who were four famous scholars and artists at that time. They appeared together on the square during the '89 protest, and stood on the students' side. At that time they were called *si junzi*." In Confucian tradition, *junzi* are what all learned people should aspire to be, and thus calling these quartets *junzi* is a show of respect.

---

3. Wukan refers to the protests that erupted in the Guangdong village in 2011 (see blockade, page 169).

4. Liu Xiaobo, Zhou Duo, Gao Xin, and Hou Dejian, four prominent public figures (Liu was a literary critic, Zhou an economist, Gao an editor, and Hou a musician) who famously joined the student protesters at Tiananmen Square in June of 1989.

翻墙

(**over the Great Firewall** / *fānqiáng*) literally means crossing the wall, but is commonly translated as "climbing over the Great Firewall"—that is, evading the network of technical controls by which China regulates foreign Internet content.

Why it is blocked: China doesn't deny that the Internet is tightly controlled in the country—with specific websites like Facebook and Twitter blocked, "immoral" content like pornography restricted, search results filtered, and individual blog posts containing politically sensitive material deleted. In fact, China openly admits and defends its Internet regulations. However, criticizing this system is not acceptable.[5] A number of tools allow netizens to circumvent the blocks to non-Chinese websites, giving them unfettered access to the outside Internet.[6] The U.S. government has been involved with funding some of these tools, including the controversial Falun Gong–designed Ultrasurf (see page 40).

According to a 2010 survey, most "climbers" over the Great Firewall are university students who simply want to use Google's

---

5. Fun fact: Though references to the Great Firewall are blocked on Weibo, those to Fang Binxing, the vilified architect and grand designer of it, are not. He was forced to close his Weibo account after irate Internet users showered him with abuse. The vitriol for him even extended into real life, when a student threw a shoe at him and became a folk hero for it. Xiao Qiang, "Fang Binxing Shoegate: Responses Within China," *China Digital Times*, May 20, 2011, chinadigitaltimes.net/2011/05/fang-binxing-shoegate-twitter-responses.

6. If you want to climb *inside* the Great Firewall and experience life as a Chinese Internet user, you can install China Channel, a Firefox browser add-on: chinachannel .fffff.at (the older Firefox version 3 is required).

7. Oiwan Lam, "China: Over the GFW," *Global Voices Advocacy*, April 30, 2010, advocacy.globalvoicesonline.org/2010/04/30/china-over-the-gfw.

search engine.[7] Other findings suggest that only a small share of Chinese Internet users bother to use anticensorship tools and are mostly satisfied with the domestic offerings available to them. However, even those compliant users can be passively involved in anticensorship efforts when they engage in practices such as using coded language on social media sites to evade censors (see river crab, page 203).

无界网络

(**Ultrasurf** / *Wújiè wǎngluò*) is a free tool for circumventing Internet censorship. Ultrasurf, also known as Ultrareach, enables Internet users in China to bypass China's Great Firewall, and now has as many as 11 million users worldwide.

Why it is blocked: Besides the fact that the software punches a hole through China's noted Great Firewall, it is also a product designed by the Falun Gong,[8] a banned Chinese religion that Chinese officials claim is a cult, and funded by the U.S. government,[9] making it even more sensitive.

There have been allegations by software experts that Ultrasurf may actually be malicious software[10] (or at the very least it exhibits behavior that appears suspicious, for instance attempting to connect surreptitiously to websites without the user's knowledge).[11] These claims are difficult to refute because the source code has not been released (supposedly in order to prevent Chinese government analysis). In April 2012, an examination of the software by Tor

---

8. Vince Beiser, "Digital Weapons Help Dissidents Punch Holes in China's Great Firewall," *Wired*, November 1, 2010, www.wired.com/magazine/2010/11/ff_firewall fighters/all/1.

9. Ultrasurf is just one of many Internet circumvention tools that the United States has supported and funded in the name of free speech. John Pomfret, "U.S. Risks China's Ire with Decision to Fund Software Maker Tied to Falun Gong," *Washington Post*, May 12, 2010, www.washingtonpost.com/wp-dyn/content/article/2010/05/11/AR2010051105154_pf.html.

10. "Ultrasurf Is Malware," Wilders Security Forum, March 25, 2009, www.wilders security.com/showthread.php?s=124c4b0360d7174ba80126f259ea08ff&t=237184.

11. Tim Greene, "Black Hat: Free Cloaking Software May Actually Draw Attention to Traffic It's Supposed to Protect," *Network World*, July 31, 2009, www.network world.com/news/2009/073109-blackhat-ultrasurf.html.

concluded that Ultrasurf was secretly monitoring users' Internet browsing.[12] As mentioned, it has been funded in part by the U.S. government, and the Berkman Center at Harvard lauded its performance back in 2007, favorably comparing its ability to circumvent censorship blocks to other similar tools.[13]

12. Jacob Appelbaum, "Ultrasurf: The Definitive Review," *Tor Blog*, April 16, 2012, blog.torproject.org/blog/ultrasurf-definitive-review.

13. Hal Roberts, Ethan Zuckerman, and John Palfrey, "2007 Circumvention Landscape Report: Methods, Uses, and Tools," Berkman Center for Internet & Society, March 5, 2009, cyber.law.harvard.edu/publications/2009/2007 _Circumvention_Landscape_Report.

(**Combining Cyrillic Millions**) is a Cyrillic character used to represent 1 million. It can also be used to initiate backward writing while typing on a computer,[14] which is helpful for languages that read from right to left, such as Arabic and Hebrew.

Why it is blocked: An anonymous Tumblr user writes: "This is called 菊花文.[15] It was mainly used for obfuscation or censorship circumvention." Essentially, running text with sensitive words through online conversion tools[16] that utilize the Cyrillic character's special technical capability allows a user to mask sensitive words from automated censorship detectors. A user will be able to post the text and another user will be able to decipher it fairly easily, but computer censors will not be able to uncover the message's meaning, so it can be read only by a human censor.

Another anonymous Tumblr user posits a different theory: "This sign is so similar to the symbol of Falun Gong or it could be possibly used as the sign online." The Falun Gong is a banned religion in China that gained notoriety when in April 1999 more than ten thousand practitioners appeared in front of the Zhongnanhai compound (a complex of government buildings that serves as the seat and symbol of the Communist Party government, akin to the White House in America) to protest discrimination against the group. Such a show of collective force, even if it was nonviolent, spooked the government, and suppression of the group was stepped up.

14. Mike Shade, "WTF Is This Character?" *Tip o' the Day*, August 26, 2007, tipothe day.com/2007/08/26/wtf-is-this-character.

15. "Chrysanthemum writing" because the symbol resembles the petals of a chrysanthemum flower.

16. You can try it out at the following site: 火星文工具, 52hxw.com, accessed December 17, 2012, tool.52hxw.com/028.html.

Falun Gong is now best known in America for its stridently anti-Communist message (see Sujiatun, page 132, and Wang Wenyi, page 105) spread via its media affiliates like the *Epoch Times*, and for its protests in front of Chinese consulate buildings.

Fun fact: 屄 and 尻 (cunt / *bī*) are the only one-character words besides the surnames of Hu Jintao (胡) and Xi Jinping (习) that I discovered to have been blocked on Weibo for significant periods of time in 2012.

维基揭密 /
維基揭密

(WikiLeaks / *Wéijījiēmì*) is an online organization that publishes secret and classified material obtained from anonymous news sources, news leaks, and whistle-blowers. 维基 is a transliteration of "Wiki," while the last two characters can be written in various ways, [17] all of which roughly mean "uncovering/explaining secrets."

Why it is blocked: China, like the United States, is deathly afraid of government leaks. Already WikiLeaks has revealed Chinese willingness to abandon its support for North Korea, and other embarrassing (if true) rumors such as Wen Jiabao's "disgust" with his wife's corruption.[18]

---

17. Both the above simplified and traditional versions have roughly the same number of Google hits. Swaps for the third and fourth characters are common. "Jie" can be written as 解, meaning "explain," or 揭, meaning "uncover." "Mi" can be written as 秘, meaning "secret," or 密, meaning "dense" (put together, 秘密 form the word "secret"). Some of these alternative variations—for instance 维基解密, apparently the most popular way to translate WikiLeaks, with roughly 9 million Google hits opposed to fewer than 1 million for the two above blocked versions—are unblocked. Such inconsistency in blocks demonstrates that Weibo censorship is not totally systematic and that "errors" such as these do still crop up.

18. Samuel Wade, "Wikileaks: From Xi Jinping's Rise to Jiang Zemin's Buddhism," *China Digital Times*, June 21, 2011, chinadigitaltimes.net/2011/06/wikileaks-from-xi-jinpings-rise-to-jiang-zemins-buddhism.

国新办

(abbreviation for 国务院新闻办公室, **State Council Information Office** (SCIO) / *Guówùyuàn Xīnwén Bàngōngshì*) is a cabinetlike department in the State Council.[19] It serves as a sort of Chinese government PR office, tasked with organizing state press conferences and performing a media-oversight role. The SCIO is distinct from the more well-known Propaganda Department, which is an internal division of the Communist Party that is informally—but often in fact—in charge of controlling how the Party's policies and messages are broadcast throughout domestic media, and the State Administration of Radio, Film, and Television (SARFT), which operates like the FCC in the United States and issues guidelines for what content is allowable. Other State Council agencies with a hand in regulating media include the General Administration of Press and Publication (GAPP) and the Ministry of Culture.[20]

Why it is blocked: In May 2011, the SCIO issued a statement announcing the initiation of the new State Internet Information Office (SIIO). The SIIO would not only handle the mundane tasks

---

19. The State Council is the administrative branch of the Chinese government and carries out day-to-day government activities. It is composed of twenty-five ministries and numerous other government organizations and commissions, for example the Ministry of Foreign Affairs, the Ministry of Justice, the National Bureau of Statistics, and so on. Though the Chinese government contains a number of other organs, in practice, the other two primary branches of power are the political branch, that is the Chinese Communist Party, and the military branch, the People's Liberation Army. In theory, these three branches potentially establish a separation of powers in government, but because they share overlapping membership, the three more often than not work as an interlocked whole.
20. In March 2013, the State Council began to take steps to consolidate redundant departments when it merged GAPP with SARFT, among other changes.

of allocating IP addresses and supervising online content, but also would have an enforcement and security arm: "It is assigned the duties to investigate and punish websites violating laws and regulations."[21] Though it is unclear whether the SIIO will take over for the myriad agencies that are already involved with regulating the Internet (in addition to the above, there's also the Ministry of Industry and Information Technology, the Ministry of Public Security, the Ministry of Commerce, and the State Administration for Industry and Commerce), based on the leadership appointments (both the director and the vice director come from the SCIO), this new agency would draw heavily from the SCIO's already established organization.

Tip for living in a place that censors content: Don't talk publicly about the people who censor your content.[22]

---

21. Xinhua, "China Sets Up State Internet Information Office," *China Daily*, May 4, 2011, www.chinadaily.com.cn/china/2011-05/04/content_12440782.htm.

22. Here's a fun one for the literary fans out there: Ministry of Truth (真理部 / *Zhēnlǐ Bù*), the fictitious department in charge of propaganda in George Orwell's *1984*, is also blocked on Weibo. Anne Henochowicz, "Word of the Week: Ministry of Truth," *China Digital Times*, August 15, 2012, chinadigitaltimes.net/2012/08/word-of-the -week-ministry-of-truth.

民主墙

(**Democracy Wall** / *Mínzhǔ Qiáng*) was a one-hundred-meter-long, two-meter-high brick wall on Xidan Street in Beijing, which was the site of public dissent in 1978 and 1979. For more than a year, citizens posted big-character posters[23] and other signs along the wall.

Why it is blocked: Though the Democracy Wall arose because of a relaxation of restrictions on criticisms of the government during the so-called Beijing Spring of 1977–78, it ended the same way Mao's Hundred Flowers Campaign[24] did: with arrests and suppression. The most well-known dissident, the activist Wei Jingsheng, who called for democracy to be the "Fifth Modernization"[25] and criticized Deng Xiaoping in a signed essay on the wall (most posters were anonymous), was imprisoned until 1997. Thus, references to the Democracy Wall elicit memories of criticisms of the authorities as well as of the duplicity of the Chinese government.

---

23. The posting of "big character posters"—that is, large written banners and papers—was one of the "four great rights" or the "four bigs." Along with the freedom to speak out fully, the freedom to air views fully, and the freedom to hold great debates, the writing of big-character posters was encouraged throughout the Cultural Revolution and codified in the 1975 national constitution. Those rights were subsequently rescinded in a 1980 revision to the constitution.

24. In 1956, Mao and the CCP encouraged citizens to speak out against officials and offer suggestions to improve the government. However, after a period of criticism, Mao ordered the dissidents jailed as counterrevolutionaries, saying that he'd "enticed the snakes out of their caves" (Philip Short, *Mao: A Life* [New York: Henry Holt, 2001], 470).

25. This is a reference to Premier Zhou Enlai's 1963 call for "Four Modernizations" to improve the Chinese economy: a need to strengthen China's agriculture, industry, defense, and science/technology.

民主女神

(Goddess of Democracy / *Mínzhǔ Nǚshén*) was a thirty-three-foot-tall foam-and-papier-mâché statue erected in Tiananmen Square, Beijing, in May 1989. The statue was constructed in pieces by a group of students in a workshop at the Central Academy of Fine Arts in just four days. The pieces were then secretly transported to the square on May 29. On May 30, students completed assembling it, and it was unveiled in a ceremony at noon. As government officials had feared, its installation revived the flagging protest, and as many as three hundred thousand people returned to the square. However, the Goddess stood for just five days—facing Mao's portrait—before it was bulldozed during the army's takeover of the square on June 4.

Why it is blocked: Though the Goddess was not modeled on the Statue of Liberty as popularly thought (the creators thought that would be too pro-American, and in fact, before the design was modified, the statue was originally to be of a man leaning on a pole), the statue served as a symbol of democracy and, in its rough-hewn beauty, expressed the demonstrators' earnest hopes for China. Along with the "Tank Man" (see page 162), it became one of the iconic images of the Tiananmen Square protests.

Though the original was destroyed, numerous replicas exist around the world today, including a controversial one that now stands at the Chinese University of Hong Kong.

盘古乐队

(**Pangu** / *Pángǔ yuèduì*), also known as **PunkGod**, is a Jiangxi punk rock trio that formed in the 1990s. They take their name from 盘古, the creator of the universe in Chinese mythology.

Why it is blocked: After developing a reputation by performing songs adapted from the poems of dissident Zhang Lin, Pangu pushed the envelope by openly declaring support for Taiwanese independence (the bassist even pinned a pro-Taiwan badge to his bare chest)[26] while playing a set in the country during the 2004 Say Yes to Taiwan music festival. When it became clear that they would be detained by local authorities when they returned home, the group fled to Sweden with the help of aid groups. After gaining political asylum in Sweden, they returned to Say Yes to Taiwan in 2006 and performed another incendiary set, chanting in one song, "Fuck Beijing's Olympic fucking games!"[27] Within China, the band is remembered by punk fans with equal parts scorn and nostalgia.[28]

26. "PUNKGOD (a.k.a. PANGU)," *Island of Sound*, accessed December 16, 2012, www.islandofsound.org/friends_of_taiwan/punkgod.html.

27. Jeremy Goldkorn, "Pangu Chant Down Babylon," *Danwei*, June 1, 2006, www.danwei.org/music/pangu_chant_down_babylon.php.

28. "Chinese Dissident mp3 Downloads," *Holidarity*, May 26, 2006, holidarity.blogspot.com/2006/05/chinese-dissident-mp3-downloads.html.

維多利亞

(**Victoria** / *Wéiduōlìyà*) is a female name. Victoria is Latin for "conquer," and in Roman mythology she was the goddess of victory, equivalent to the Greek goddess Nike.

Why it is blocked: Could it be the Latin meaning? Or maybe those too sexy Victoria's Secret models? The shadow of Queen Victoria and colonial emasculation? Or . . . Posh Spice? No, rather, the word is blocked because of Victoria Park in Hong Kong (searching for 維園, the first character in Victoria, along with the character for park, is also blocked).

Every June 4, Victoria Park is the site of a candlelight vigil to commemorate those who died in the Tiananmen Square crackdown in 1989. Hundreds of thousands attend each year to hear speeches against one-party dictatorship, to sing protest songs (see "The Flower of Freedom," page 147), and to honor the victims and their families. The park is also used for other demonstrations, including serving as the meeting point for activists for the annual prodemocracy July 1 marches. Since Hong Kong uses a slightly different writing system than mainland China, of note is the fact that only the traditional characters (that is, the Hong Kong system of writing) for Victoria are blocked.[29] A search for 维多利亚, the way

---

29. In efforts to increase literacy rates, the PRC simplified a great deal of its written characters starting in the 1950s. Basically, many of the components (known as radicals) that compose characters have now been abbreviated so they take fewer strokes to write, though other characters have been left unchanged. For example, "China" has traditionally been written as 中國 (middle country/kingdom). However, the internal radical of the word "country" (the stuff inside the square) has been simplified so that you now currently write it in the simplified system as中国. However, for political and cultural reasons, places like Taiwan, Hong Kong, and many overseas Chinese communities never converted to the simplified system and continued to write and publish

a mainlander would write it, is unblocked (you'll see links relating to Victoria, Australia, and Victoria's Secret in the web page's sidebar). 維園, an abbreviation for Victoria Park, is also unsearchable in traditional characters but is unblocked when converted to simplified characters, a clear indication that the censorship is linked to the Hong Kong park.

---

with the traditional characters. Even today, Taiwan and Hong Kong citizens maintain their separate writing systems. They do this because of upbringing, personal preference, and tradition (though a young literate person might be able to read in either system, writing is usually possible only in the person's home set of characters unless he or she is especially well traveled or educated) but also in some cases as a badge of political independence and anti-Communism. Thus, blocking the traditional characters for Victoria is clearly aimed at those who would write it that way: Hong Kongers.

五月三十五

(**May 35** / *Wǔyuè sānshíwǔ*) is the imaginary thirty-fifth day of May.

Why it is blocked: May has 31 days, so May 32 would be June 1, May 33 would be June 2, May 34 would be June 3, and May 35 would be . . . June 4—the day the army was sent into Tiananmen Square in Beijing in 1989 to put down demonstrators. Because June 4 is obviously blocked (both the Arabic numbers 64 and Chinese characters for the date), numerous creative ways were derived by Internet users to circumvent censorship. 五月三十五 was one, but there were others: 四號 (day four), 六月初 (the beginning of June), "siliu" and "liusi" (phonetic translations of the words for six and four), 第四 (the fourth), 35号 (day 35), 四突擊 (literally, four assault), 四运动 (literally, four movement), 四事件 (literally, four event), 四號戰車 (day four tanks), and many more. All those listed above have been or still are blocked.

绿坝娘

(**Green Dam Girl** / *lǜbàniáng*) was an unofficial mascot for the web-filtering software Green Dam. Green Dam was heavily supported and financed by the Chinese government and was supposed to serve as a complement to the Great Firewall. While the Great Firewall would be operated by the government and perform Internet censorship at the national level, Green Dam software on each computer would more flexibly filter out anything else the user and authorities decided was objectionable. Initial statements in 2009 indicated that installation of the software would be required on all computers sold in China, but authorities reversed course and made it optional.

Why it is blocked: Green Dam was despised by Internet users, and a vast majority of netizens expressed no interest in using the product. Though it was billed as software that would protect users from pornography and other sexual content, critics claimed it would infringe on free speech, open up security vulnerabilities on users' computers, and be ineffective even for those who wanted to use the software. At the height of the Green Dam criticism in 2009, netizens even created the Green Dam Girl, an anthropomorphized stand-in for the software. Drawn in typical anime style, she wore a hat with a river crab (pronounced *héxiè* in Chinese, phonetically similar to 和谐, meaning harmonious, one of the buzzwords during the Hu Jintao administration; see page 203), clutched a brush to paint over offensive content, and carried a rabbit—the actual official mascot of Green Dam.

因言获罪

(**criminalization of speech** / *yīnyán huòzuì*) is punishment for speaking or writing thoughts that are deemed illegal or harmful.

Why it is blocked: The Chinese constitution states, "Citizens of the People's Republic of China enjoy freedom of speech, of the press, of assembly, of association, of procession, and of demonstration,"[30] and a 2010 white paper on Internet usage in China asserted, "Chinese citizens fully enjoy freedom of speech on the Internet."[31] Neither, of course, is actually true based on just about any conception of free speech,[32] though it can rightfully be argued that there are limitations on speech even in "free" countries such as the United States (see Internet monitoring, page 62). In China, an individual can be jailed for a number of speech crimes (see inciting subversion of state power, page 184), and journalists in particular are very cognizant of the limitations on the press; since the state considers control of the media and speech a key component of ensuring stability and continued progress in China, it is highly unlikely that there will be major changes to the speech

---

30. However, the article guaranteeing this is toothless and currently not enforced by courts. Brian Palmer, "Is There Freedom of Speech in China?," *Slate*, October 8, 2010, www.slate.com/articles/news_and_politics/explainer/2010/10/is_there_freedom _of_speech_in_china.html.

31. Information Office of the State Council of the People's Republic of China, "III. Guaranteeing Citizens' Freedom of Speech on the Internet," GOV.cn, June 8, 2010, english.gov.cn/2010-06/08/content_1622956.htm.

32. Internet scholars such as Rebecca MacKinnon, Xiao Qiang, and Guobin Yang discuss the limitations placed on Chinese Internet users (and the way netizens respond) in their writing, while work by researchers such as Gary King and Jedidiah R. Crandall empirically shows what kind of information is actually censored online and how those censorship mechanisms operate.

criminalization laws.[33] In a major speech in 2010, Hu Jintao noted, "Correct guidance of public opinion benefits the party, benefits the nation, and benefits the people. Incorrect guidance of public opinion wrongs the party, wrongs the nation, and wrongs the people."[34]

33. David Bandurski, "Hu Jintao Reform Blueprint Defines CCP Media Control as a Key Condition of 'Political Reform,'" China Media Project, April 18, 2008, cmp.hku.hk/2008/04/18/948.

34. David Bandurski, "Propaganda Leaders Scurry Off to Carry Out the 'Spirit' of Hu Jintao's 'Important' Media Speech," China Media Project, June 25, 2008, cmp.hku.hk/2008/06/25/1079.

宪法法院

(**constitutional court** / *xiànfǎ fǎyuàn*) is the court charged with adjudicating cases that concern the constitution. In some countries, it is distinct from a supreme court, which is the highest court in a country and the court of last resort for nonconstitutional cases. In the United States, the Supreme Court does both tasks. China's Supreme People's Court (SPC) serves as a supreme court but does not currently have the power of constitutional review.[35]

Why it is blocked: The power of the courts is a controversial issue in China. The modern Chinese court system is often a less-than-independent entity,[36] and there is no separation of powers between the courts and the state to prevent the state from abusing its authority. In recent years under Xiao Yang, the president of the Supreme People's Court from 1998 to 2008, a number of reforms held promise. In 2001, the Supreme People's Court agreed to rule on a case and decided that a student, Qi Yuling, should be awarded damages after another student stole her identity and test scores to attend college. But what made the case more interesting was not just the decision, but the argument: the court premised its ruling on

---

35. Larry Catá Backer, "A Constitutional Court for China Within the Chinese Communist Party: Scientific Development and the Institutional Role of the CCP," *Suffolk University Law Review*, Summer 2010, papers.ssrn.com//sol3/papers.cfm ?abstract_id=1308598.

36. Judges in modern China have historically had spotty legal training. Even those who are better educated often bend to political pressures in order to protect their jobs. In one famous 2003 case, Judge Li Huijuan ruled in a mundane dispute over seed prices that a provincial law contradicted national law and should not be upheld. Provincial officials went ballistic at this challenge to their lawmaking autonomy and ordered local judges to rehear the case. Huijuan, who had unwittingly set the precedent for a *Marbury v. Madison* scenario, was eventually forced out of her job.

the Chinese constitution, arguing that according to the document, Qi had the right to an education, the first time the court had asserted its ability to oversee the constitution. As the case was decidedly nonpolitical, legal scholars saw this as a gradual introduction of constitutional review into the Chinese legal system. However, those hopes were temporarily dashed after the Communist Party reasserted its power over the courts and issued a doctrine known as the "Three Supremes." It held that judges must consider political ramifications and social stability in addition to the law.[37] In 2008, Wang Shengjun, who does not have a law background, was appointed as the new president of the Supreme People's Court, and in 2009, the landmark Qi Yuling ruling was withdrawn, an indication that the SPC was stepping away from making constitutional judgments.[38]

The question of what role the courts should play and the importance of upholding China's constitution exploded at the beginning of January 2013, when the highly respected *Southern Weekend* (also known in English as *Southern Weekly*) magazine's editors objected to the editing of their annual New Year's editorial. The editorial, which concerned the need for improved constitutional rule, was replaced by a paean to the Communist Party.[39] *Southern Weekend* editors and staffers went on strike, and the drama—which involved public demonstrations by citizens, coded messages of support from media outlets and companies fed up with censorship, a teary-eyed refusal to print an editorial attacking *Southern Weekend* by its sister magazine *Beijing News*,[40] and even calls of solidarity

Jim Yardley, "A Judge Tests China's Courts, Making History," *New York Times*, November 28, 2005, www.nytimes.com/2005/11/28/international/asia/28judge.html ?pagewanted=all.

37. From a Hu Jintao speech in 2008 describing the Three Supremes: "In their work, the grand judges and grand procurators shall always regard as supreme the Party's cause, the people's interest, and the constitution and laws."

38. Thomas E. Kellogg, "The Death of Constitutional Litigation in China?," *China Brief*, Jamestown Foundation, April 2, 2009, www.jamestown.org/programs/chinabrief/single /?tx_ttnews%5Btt_news%5D=34791&tx_ttnews%5BbackPid%5D=414&no_cache=1.

39. Qian Gang, "Why Southern Weekly Said 'No,'" China Media Project, January 11, 2013, cmp.hku.hk/2013/01/11/30623.

40. "Face-Off in a Beijing Newsroom: An Insider's Account," China Real Time

from glamorous celebrities[41]—served as an inauspicious start to the Xi Jinping era. Eventually a truce was struck: *Southern Weekend* staffers returned to their offices while *Southern Weekend*'s editor and several officials either lost or will lose their jobs, reportedly including the despised Guangdong propaganda chief who started the tempest, Tuo Zhen.[42]

My records show the term has been blocked for over a year, and thus has been sensitive for some time. However, according to GreatFire.org, it was unblocked in November 2012, before becoming reblocked sometime in late December 2012—around the start of the *Southern Weekend* controversy. Perhaps the block is coincidental, but, depending on when exactly the reblock of 宪法法院 took place, one could make a credible case that it is related to the event.

Report, *Wall Street Journal* blog, January 9, 2013, blogs.wsj.com/chinarealtime/2013 /01/09/face-off-in-a-beijing-newsroom-an-insiders-account.

41. Evan Osnos, "Solzhenitsyn, Yao Chen, and Chinese Reform," Letter from China, *New Yorker* blog, January 8, 2013, www.newyorker.com/online/blogs/evanosnos/2013 /01/solzhenitsyn-yao-chen-and-battle-over-chinese-reform.html.

42. Samuel Wade, "Southern Weekly Editor Replaced to Calm Dispute," *China Digital Times*, January 18, 2013, chinadigitaltimes.net/2013/01/southern-weekly -editor-replaced-to-calm-dispute.

四二六社论

(**April 26 editorial** / *sì èr liù shèlùn*) was a front-page article printed in the *People's Daily*, the official Chinese Communist Party newspaper, on April 26, 1989. The article was penned by the Politburo Standing Committee (PSC)[43] and addressed the growing protests in Tiananmen Square. Deng Xiaoping, though not part of the PSC and not involved with writing the editorial, was consulted early on, and the article included his description of the events as 动乱 (*dòngluàn*), meaning disturbance or turmoil, in the title and six more times in the article. This was done in an effort to paint the demonstrators as a harmful, destabilizing force.

Why it is blocked: The description of the protests and students as inciting turmoil was a point of contention throughout the weeks of the Tiananmen protest. The students strongly objected to their demonstrations being described as disturbances and feared that if the notion took hold, they would lose their moral high ground and the support of citizens across the country. On May 18, student leaders met with former premier Li Peng, the most prominent advocate of a hard line against the students, in a nationally televised broadcast to demand that the government retract the editorial as a precondition for ending their hunger strike.[44] The government rejected the

---

43. Zhao Ziyang's memoir, *Prisoner of State* (New York: Simon & Schuster, 2010), details his attempts to convince his peers to tone down the hard-line nature of the editorial. In the months leading up to June 4, he was stripped of his power, and after the crackdown he was purged from the Party. He lived out the rest of his life under house arrest.

44. The hunger strike, one component of the protests, was generating a great amount of negative publicity for the government. The students were able to sway the emotions of parents across the country to their cause and convince them of the government's

request and both sides hardened their positions. Unfortunately, the editorial's claim of "turmoil" was self-fulfilling. Having already labeled the demonstrators as troublemakers, the editorial helped provide the pretext for the government to forcefully shut down the protest, leading to the violence of June 4.

negligence in ignoring their demands. "Li Peng Holds Dialogue with Students," Long Bow Group, accessed December 16, 2012, www.tsquare.tv/chronology/May18mtg .html.

60

网络评论员

(**Internet commentators** / *wǎngluò pínglùnyuán*) is a seemingly benign phrase and one might assume it is blocked due to the power of netizens. However, it is actually an ironic, derogatory name for the professional and volunteer members of the 50 Cent Party (see page 36), that is, people who post positive comments about China and Communist Party policy on message boards, microblogs, blogs, and news articles at a proverbial rate of fifty cents per post.

Why it is blocked: For the same reason that 50 Cent Party is blocked: don't talk about the government's stranglehold on the media.

网络监控

(**Internet monitoring** / *wǎngluò jiānkòng*) refers to China's extensive system of structural, social, and legal controls by which it regulates the Internet (see 50 Cent Party, page 36, and over the Great Firewall, page 38).

Why it is blocked: Every country—even Western, free-speech-loving ones—has its own manner of regulating speech and information online, often in the name of protecting its citizens from terrorism or crime, or for other legal reasons.[45]

While one can argue about whether these sorts of controls in America and Europe constitute censorship or merely a lack of total privacy, the consensus is that China's Internet-monitoring policies are much more severe—and sometimes have harsh, real-life consequences for Chinese citizens (see criminalization of speech, page 54). In 2004, the journalist Shi Tao leaked a government e-mail to

---

45. Recognizing the importance of protecting intellectual property in the digital age, America sought to develop laws that would defend artists and content creators from online piracy. Unfortunately, the end product in 1998 was the much-maligned Digital Millennium Copyright Act (DMCA), which was exploited by the music recording industry to sue individuals for incredible sums of money for allegedly sharing songs online. Before the DMCA, record companies were not able to tie copyright infringement that they detected online to a specific person; after the DMCA, they were able to subpoena the identity of an individual from the user's Internet provider ("RIAA v. the People: Five Years Later," Electronic Frontier Foundation, September 30, 2008, www.eff.org/wp/riaa-v-people-five-years-later). This sort of personally identifying data is collected by all Internet providers now and is liable to be shared with law enforcement and companies due to the passage of the DMCA; the Patriot Act ("Module V—Governmental Collection of Data—Part II: USA Patriot and Foreign Intelligence Surveillance," Berkman Center for Internet & Society, Fall 2003, cyber .law.harvard.edu/privacy/module5.html); and the Foreign Intelligence Surveillance

a New York organization. Authorities traced the leak to a Yahoo! e-mail account, and after compelling the company to release the identity of the e-mailer, they arrested Shi and sentenced him to ten years in prison.[46] In 2010, a woman was sentenced to a year in a labor camp for sharing a Twitter post (see page 142).[47] Such reactions serve as deterrents to other Internet users and warnings that they should censor themselves lest they be caught by those watching their conversations.

Act (Rainey Reitman, "Stop Congress from Reauthorizing the FISA Amendments Act, a Warrantless Spying Bill," Electronic Frontier Foundation, December 13, 2012, www.eff.org/deeplinks/2012/12/congress-poised-reauthorize-fisa-amendment-act -warrantless-spying-bill). These and other, similar laws allow the government to monitor Internet users, suppress the sharing or transmission of certain information online, and punish those who break these laws. This is in addition to run-of-the-mill Internet monitoring that most websites and Internet browsers employ to track and serve ads more effectively to Internet users.

46. Activists and Western politicians pilloried Yahoo! for its act, comparing Yahoo! to a police informant. To its credit, Yahoo! tried to rectify its mistake, and the company has since campaigned for Shi's release. In 2008, a number of companies led by Yahoo!, Google, and Microsoft formed the Global Network Initiative, an NGO that pledged to protect the privacy of online users and obliged participating companies to prevent another Shi Tao case from ever happening.

47. Damian Grammaticas, "Chinese Woman Jailed over Twitter Post," BBC, November 18, 2010, www.bbc.co.uk/news/world-asia-pacific-11784603.

3

#sex# #drugs# #immorality#

一夜情

(**one-night stand** / yīyèqíng) originally described a single theater performance, usually by a guest performer on tour. Today, however, the term is more commonly used to mean a single sexual encounter, in which neither participant has any intention or expectation of an ongoing relationship.

Why it is blocked: Sex is a touchy subject in China—though you wouldn't necessarily know it from talking to young Chinese folks or from reading classic Chinese novels like the erotic *The Plum in the Golden Vase* (*Jin Ping Mei*). An article in the *People's Daily* about a sex toy exhibition gets at some of the contradictions regarding sex in contemporary China. Though the business manager of the event admitted that "sex and adult products are a sensitive topic in China. We are a little worried about the reaction from the audience," sex toy sales are reported to be thriving. And yet, a survey mentioned in that same article revealed that only 21 percent of men surveyed knew where the clitoris was located on the female body.[1]

China has historically been quite accepting of what some might consider deviant sexual behavior, with frank discussions of homosexuality, concubines, prostitution, and the pleasure of sex found in traditional texts and historical accounts. But things changed markedly in the twentieth century, first with the Nationalist Kuomintang (KMT) efforts during the New Life Movement of the 1930s to promote good citizen behavior—which included the censoring of scenes of sexual impropriety in movies—and then again after the

---

1. "Adult Sex Toy Expo Touches Sensitive Area," *Shanghai Star*, *People's Daily* online, August 8, 2004, english.peopledaily.com.cn/200408/08/eng20040808_152209 .html.

Communist Revolution in the 1950s.[2] Mao decided that in order to strengthen families and build the best society possible, it would be best go on the attack against deviant sexual behaviors.[3] "Anti–spiritual pollution" campaigns took place periodically over the next three decades, with pornography being a prime target for attack.

Though many conservative sexual norms remain in contemporary China—for instance, virginity among women is still prized, premarital sex is still looked down upon by the older generation, and distributing pornography is still a crime[4]—China has undergone an opening up of its sexual behaviors. Homosexuality was decriminalized in 1997 and the government now views sex shops and phone sex lines as potential avenues for improving mental health.[5] However, as evidenced by the blocked words in this chapter, the government and Weibo still view sexuality as a sensitive topic, to be treated with caution.

---

2. Zhiwei Xiao, "The Myth About Chinese Leftist Cinema," in *Visualizing Modern China*, ed. James A. Cook, Joshua Goldstein, and Sigrid Schmalzer (Lanham, MD: Rowman & Littlefield, forthcoming).

3. Mao was a huge hypocrite regarding sex. At the same time he was legislating and speaking out against nontraditional sexual behavior, he was famously engaging in sex with a whole harem of young women. His sexual excesses have been fodder for books including *The Private Life of Chairman Mao*, a memoir by Li Zhisui, one of Mao's personal doctors (New York: Random House, 1996).

4. "China Arrests Thousands in Latest Internet Crime Crackdown," BBC, July 26, 2012, www.bbc.co.uk/news/technology-18996811.

5. James T. Areddy, "The Shifting Terrain of Sex in China," China Real Time Report, *Wall Street Journal* blog, October 17, 2012, blogs.wsj.com/chinarealtime/2012/10/17/the-shifting-terrain-of-sex-in-china.

尤物

(literally, **outstanding thing** / *yóuwù*) is translated by some dictionaries as "**rare beauty**." What the thing is depends on the author's usage. In some traditional poetry, 尤物 could describe a stunning nature landscape, but in the Warring States Period book *Zuo Zhuan* (circa 389 BCE), the phrase was used to describe an extremely beautiful but wicked girl.[6] This usage is most common today: a physically gorgeous woman.

Why it is blocked: Searching for pictures of beautiful, especially nude, girls online corrupts individual morals and destroys the fabric of society—according to Chinese authorities, that is.

In June 1983, the would-be defender of the student protesters in Tiananmen, Zhao Ziyang (see April 26 editorial, page 59, note 43), decried the increasing amount of crime in Chinese society and blamed relaxed moral codes among writers, artists, and others taking advantage of China's opening up. He called for law enforcement to crack down on such "ideological apathy," and in October, with Deng Xiaoping's blessing, the Anti–Spiritual Pollution Campaign of 1983 thus commenced. Excessive individualism, materialistic behavior, Western fashion, and pornography were criticized on streets and in the press. Though the campaign ended just two months later, its effects carried on through the years with intermittent calls by officials and media to beat back encroaching Western values. Internet pornography was banned in 2002, and the govern-

---

6. Anne Kinney, "Book X. Duke Zhao," *Traditions of Exemplary Women*, accessed December 17, 2012, www2.iath.virginia.edu/saxon/servlet/SaxonServlet?source =xwomen/texts/chunqiu.xml&style=xwomen/xsl/dynaxml.xsl&chunk.id=d2.16&toc .depth=1&toc.id=0&doc.lang=bilingual.

ment reaffirmed the prohibition in a 2010 State Council Information Office (see page 45) white paper on Internet regulation.[7]

Today, performing a web search for 尤物 returns images of scantily clad and nude women. Like 黄色 (yellow / *huángsè*)[8] or "XXX" in English—which originally was used as a mark on casks of beer to "convey an impression of its extra strength"[9]—the term now carries this additional titillating connotation (especially online) in addition to its original meaning.

7. Information Office of the State Council of the People's Republic of China, "IV. Basic Principles and Practices of Internet Administration," GOV.cn, June 8, 2010, english.gov.cn/2010-06/08/content_1622956.htm.

8. A user on *Stack Exchange* cites a Chinese article that presents four possible explanations for how "yellow" came to be slang for pornography, though none are definitive. ("How Did 黄 (Yellow) Come to Mean 'Pornographic'?," *Stack Exchange*, January 8, 2013, chinese.stackexchange.com/questions/2673/how-did-%E9%BB%83 -yellow-come-to-mean-pornographic.) The most commonly given explanation is that at some point, either historically in China or during the nineteenth century in France, erotic books were given either yellow covers or interiors to set them apart, and thus yellow came to be closely associated with pornography.

9. "What's the Origin of 'XXX,' as in Porn Movies and Booze?," *Straight Dope*, December 17, 2012, www.straightdope.com/columns/read/1628/whats-the-origin-of -xxx-as-in-porn-movies-and-booze.

换妻

(literally, **switch wives** / *huànqī*) is the consensual activity where sexual partners are swapped. Though in English it's commonly now referred to with the gender-neutral terms **swinging** or **partner swapping**, the Chinese term 换妻, best translated as "wife swapping," still carries the male-dominated point of view.

Why it is blocked: Partner-swapping orgies are technically illegal in China based on a 1997 law banning "group licentiousness." Ringleaders of such activities are subject to a prison term of up to five years. In fact, China under the Communist Party has a history of trying to control sex and morals through the law. A 1979 law actually criminalized "hooliganism," a class of sexual crimes including adultery, premarital sex, and engaging in sex acts with multiple partners at the same time. This draconian law was replaced by the 1997 law banning "group licentiousness." This vague law came to the notice of Western media when a twice-divorced computer science professor, Ma Yaohai, was sentenced to three and a half years in jail after refusing to plead guilty to organizing more than eighteen sex orgies. Though he admitted to the acts, he said, "How can I disturb social order? What happens in my house is a private matter."[10]

Another group-sex controversy erupted in August 2012 when Weibo users started circulating leaked photos of three middle-aged men and three younger women having group sex. It was purported that one of the men was Wang Mingsheng, the Party head of a district in Anhui Province, and another was his deputy. Wang denied his involvement, but netizens reacted harshly anyway, believing it to be another sign of government officials acting with impunity.

---

10. Edward Wong, "18 Orgies Later, Chinese Swinger Gets Prison Bed," *New York Times*, May 20, 2010, www.nytimes.com/2010/05/21/world/asia/21china.html.

性交

(**sexual intercourse** / *xìngjiāo*) is a term used in sex-related words, including 近親性交 (incest / *jìnqīn xìngjiāo*), 性交体位 (sexual positions / *xìngjiāo tǐwèi*), 三人性交 (threesome / *sānrén xìngjiāo*), and others, all of which are banned. Some other words for intercourse are also banned, including the innocent-sounding 作爱 (*zuò'ài*), which literally means "make love."

Why it is blocked: Some things haven't changed since 2004, when 性交 was discovered to be blocked on Chinese instant messaging programs.[11] Anne-Marie Brady notes that of those words revealed to be banned, a third of them were sex-related, "reflecting the strong ban on pornography in China and the dominance of pornographic websites on the world wide web."[12] A cursory test shows that a number of those words are still blocked on Weibo, though some critics contend that doesn't stop young folks from using the service for lascivious purposes.[13]

---

11. Xiao Qiang, "A List of Censored Words in Chinese Cyberspace," *China Digital Times*, August 30, 2004, chinadigitaltimes.net/2004/08/the-words-you-never-see-in-chinese-cyberspace.

12. Anne-Marie Brady, *Marketing Dictatorship: Propaganda and Thought Work in Contemporary China* (Lanham, MD: Rowman & Littlefield, 2008), 135.

13. In an interview about the power of social media, the Chinese celebrity blogger Han Han declared (perhaps tongue in cheek), "In China, I think if not for social media, many casual sexual activities would suffer delays." Channel NewsAsia, "Conversation with Han Han," YouTube, September 21, 2011, www.youtube.com/watch?feature=player_detailpage&v=gnM-XES3dRw#t=1284s.

(**meow** / *mīmī*) is onomatopoeia for a cat mewing. It's also an oboelike instrument featured in the folk music of regions including Gansu and Qinghai Provinces; a nickname for a cat; a Western name (e.g., Mimi from *La bohème*); and, most relevantly for us, slang for breasts (roughly equivalent to "**tits**" in English).

Why it is blocked: This word should be filed under sex, pornography, and spiritual pollution (see rare beauty, page 68). One can't help being amused at the kinds of issues the central authorities feel are necessary to govern (in order to pursue a harmonious and moral society) and Weibo considers necessary to block (in order not to run afoul of those central authorities).

六合彩

(**Mark Six** / *liùhécăi*) is a lottery organized in Hong Kong. Mark Six is akin to the Pick-6 lotteries in the United States.

Why it is blocked: The general word for lottery (彩票 / *căipiào*) is unblocked, though this regional Cantonese version played in Hong Kong is blocked. All gambling was officially banned by the Communist Party in 1949 for its immoral and purported colonial influences (despite the fact that China has a long history of gambling, including supposedly having "invented" the state lottery, with keno slips from the Chinese Han Dynasty believed to have helped finance the building of the Great Wall). However, cracks began to show when China instituted a pair of state lotteries for the public welfare in 1987[14] and permitted horse betting in Wuhan in 2003.[15] As for why the Hong Kong version is targeted but not these other lotteries, one can only guess.

14. Li Xiang, "Gambling Still a Fact of Chinese Life," *China Daily*, April 27, 2009, www.chinadaily.com.cn/bw/2009-04/27/content_7717886.htm.
15. Chen Xiaorong, "Wuhan Bids to Revive Betting at the Racetrack," *China Daily*, April 27, 2009, www.chinadaily.com.cn/business/2009-04/27/content_7719664.htm.

露点

(**dew point** / *lùdiǎn*) is the temperature at which air must be cooled in order for water vapor to condense into liquid.

Why it is blocked: Certainly not for its scientific meaning. An alternative meaning for 露 is "reveal" or "expose." 点 can mean not only "point" but also "a little." Thus, it is slang for "reveal a bit (of skin)" or, translated more loosely into English, something like "nipple slip" or "crotch shot." Based on news references and searches on Google, the term can be used for both accidental cases and intentional exposures (e.g., risqué photo shoots).

Note: A similar word, 暴露 (expose, reveal, or bare / *bàolù*), is used in the same way as 露点. A noun form, 暴露癖 (*bàolùpǐ*), is equivalent to "exhibitionism" or "flashing." This is also blocked.

春药

(**aphrodisiac** / *chūnyào*) or 媚药 (*mèiyào*) is a substance that increases sexual desire. Examples of natural aphrodisiacs are ginseng, chocolate, and deer penis wine (at least in some Asian countries today).

Why it is blocked: Even though China has a long history of using aphrodisiacs (purportedly even emperors relied on them to "satisfy" their harems of concubines), certain discussions about improving one's virility are apparently taboo.[16] Perhaps this is a public safety measure, what with reports of older sex-pill-popping lotharios dying after engaging in overly vigorous sex sessions.[17] In 2011, a strange rumor cropped up about an aphrodisiac made of dead babies being sold in China. Though the rumor didn't appear to go viral in the mainland (it mostly showed up in overseas media), perhaps the block is related to it.[18] More likely, the block is due to general touchiness about discussing sexual matters in Chinese media.

---

16. However, Viagra (伟哥 / *wěigē*) is not blocked.

17. Also, in *Jin Ping Mei*, one of China's most famous novels, a character dies of an accidental overdose of aphrodisiac pills.

18. Matthew Robertson, "Dead Babies Used to Make Pills in China, South Korean Network Says," Eye on China, *Epoch Times*, August 6, 2011, blog.theepochtimes.com /1/china/2011/08/06/dead-babies-used-to-make-pills-in-china-korean-network-says.

恋足

(**foot fetish** / *liànzú*) is a sexual interest in feet.

Why it is blocked: As seen in this chapter, words related to sex, especially "perverse" sexual acts, are sensitive. However, perhaps Weibo realized that it was being overly cautious, as a number of these words, including "foot fetish," were unblocked in 2012.

裸照

(nude photograph / luǒzhào) is . . . well, a nude photograph. 床照 (literally, bed photo / *chuángzhào*) is a photograph of oneself or one's partner while in a sexual situation.

Why it is blocked: One of the most infamous events of the past decade in China involved the leaking of nude photographs of Hong Kong pop star Edison Chen with a number of female celebrities in 2008. The media coverage in Hong Kong was overwhelming, with newspapers devoting front-page headlines to the scandal. Police in both mainland China and Hong Kong tried to halt distribution of the photos, threatening to arrest people who just downloaded the images. In the end, the government was mostly powerless to stop the spread, as magazines, homemade bootleg DVDs, and online message boards all shared the photos.

无毛

(literally, **without hair** / *wúmáo*) can be used to describe any hairless thing (including animals) but is usually used to refer to a woman's hairless pubic region, more vulgarly known in English as a shaved pussy.

Why it is blocked: Rather than being an implicit moral judgment of one's grooming habits, this is likely blocked because it is a term used to look for pornography, a totally separate immoral activity. Alternatively, perhaps it might be used as a homophone (it is pronounced with similar syllables) for the 50 Cent Party (see page 36).

裤袜

(**panty hose**, **stockings**, or **tights** / *kùwà*), literally "pants sock" in Chinese, is legwear made of nylon or spandex typically worn by women for fashion or comfort. It was popularized by skirt-wearing women in the United States and the United Kingdom who were required by social conventions not to show their bare legs in public or in the office.

Why it is blocked: Probably because image search results for 裤袜 are too sexy for somebody's taste.

人吃人

(literally, **people eat people** / *rén chī rén*) is a reference to cases of cannibalism, the practice of eating the flesh or organs of one's own species.

Why it is blocked: This is unclear. Although there is some documentation that ritualistic cannibalism was performed during the Tang Dynasty, the most noted acts of cannibalism in Chinese history occurred during the Great Famine, which began in 1958. Recent books detailing such cases, which reached the extent that parents would trade children (so they wouldn't have to eat their own child), and where human flesh was openly sold in the market, include Frank Dikötter's *Mao's Great Famine*, Jasper Becker's *Hungry Ghosts*, and Yang Jisheng's *Tombstone*.

As the phrase being blocked is colloquial and not the standard official term (同类相食 / *tóng lèi xiāng shí*), it's likely it is censored for reasons unrelated to the Great Famine. The case of a Yunnan man named Zhang Yongming, dubbed the "cannibal monster," made news in the summer of 2012. He was convicted of strangling eleven boys and young men over three years and selling their flesh. However, the term was blocked as far back as November 2011, but unblocked throughout 2012, so it's unlikely to be connected to this, either. Similarly, the Hong Kong TV drama *When Heaven Burns*, about a group that gets trapped on a mountain and must eat one of their party, made headlines in December 2011 when authorities ordered that mainland broadcasters pull the show from the air. Again, the block predates that censorship, so it may just be Weibo's general aversion to the sharing of such heinous acts and not connected to any specific news event.

女同

(**lesbian** / *nǚtong*) is a term used to describe female homosexuality.

Why it is blocked: Homosexuality, though long accepted in traditional Chinese culture, was harshly punished during the Cultural Revolution. In 1997, China decriminalized homosexuality, and that same year the Chinese Society of Psychiatry retracted a 1989 classification of homosexuality as a mental disorder. And more recently, in July 2012, the Chinese Ministry of Health lifted a ban on lesbians giving blood. Though homophobia still exists in China, gay and lesbian rights groups are growing more active, and the government has advocated a neutral position on homosexuality commonly known as the Triple No Policy: no approval, no disapproval, no promotion.

The reason the term "lesbian" was blocked (it's now been unblocked) probably has to do with a far more prosaic—or more salacious, depending on your view—reason: to prevent people from finding and sharing lesbian pornography.

七宗罪

(**seven deadly sins** / *qī zōng zuì*) are a category of vices that according to Catholic teachings threaten a person with eternal damnation. They are wrath, greed, sloth, pride, lust, envy, and gluttony.

Why it is blocked: Touchiness with Christianity and Catholicism (see Sacred Heart Cathedral, page 204)? Upholding morals by not exposing netizens to such wicked knowledge? Or maybe just a misguided attempt to prevent anyone from attempting to re-create the series of murders and tortures in the 1995 David Fincher film *Se7en* (translated as 七宗罪 in China and Hong Kong)?

近親相姦

(**incest** / *jìnqīn xiāngjiān*) refers to sexual relations between close relatives or family members.

Why it is blocked: Like some other countries, China does not have a national law that punishes consensual sex between relatives, but incest isn't particularly common in contemporary China. Traditionally, even marrying a person with the same surname as yours was not encouraged—a not-uncommon issue considering that the top ten surnames in China are borne by over 40 percent of the population.[19] That custom has been relaxed in recent times so long as it's known the partners are not related. Incest, like other unconventional sexual practices, is clearly not encouraged by a government that seeks to build a society that is not spiritually polluted. But then again, does the government truly think users might take to Weibo to celebrate and share posts about incest?

---

19. As of 2006, they are 王 (*Wáng*), 李 (*Lǐ*), 张 (*Zhāng*), 刘 (*Liú*), 陈 (*Chén*), 杨 (*Yáng*), 黄 (*Huáng*), 赵 (*Zhào*), 吴 (*Wú*), and 周 (*Zhōu*).

大麻

(**marijuana** / *dàmá*) can refer both to hemp and to smokable cannabis. It grows naturally throughout southwestern China and is harvested for rope manufacturing. It has also been used throughout Chinese history as an anesthetic and medicine. Today, it is illegally cultivated in Xinjiang and Yunnan for the global and domestic drug trade.

Why it is blocked: China has among the strictest antidrug laws in the world—it appears the memory of the opium addicts of the nineteenth century is strong—with drug traffickers occasionally put to death, usually to "celebrate" the United Nations' annual Antidrug Day.[20] Marijuana is no exception, though the amount of marijuana seized by authorities each year pales in comparison to the amounts of heroin[21] and precursor chemicals that are used to produce synthetic drugs like methamphetamine. It's hard to pin down just how big a problem drug abuse is in China (the UN Office on Drugs and Crime reports that the number of registered heroin users in China rose to 1.1 million in 2010, which is 70 percent of all heroin users in East Asia[22]), but authorities typically blame foreigners for China's drug problem. One particular location of interest is Sanlitun, the bar district in Beijing. Police raids on expatriate clubs and bars take

---

20. Otherwise known as the International Day Against Drug Abuse and Illicit Trafficking, June 26 each year. "International Day Against Drug Abuse and Illicit Trafficking," United Nations, accessed December 17, 2012, www.un.org/en/events /drugabuseday.

21. Heroin (海洛因 / *hǎiluòyīn*, or 白粉 / *báifěn*, among other names) has been blocked at various times, as has meth (冰毒 / *bīngdú*).

22. Sam Holmes, "Opium Rebounds on China Demand," *Wall Street Journal*, November 1, 2012, online.wsj.com/article/SB100014240529702047071045780906142 85930862.html.

place periodically, with police detaining and deporting foreigners carrying illicit drugs.[23] However, drug abuse, particularly of meth, is spreading beyond the typical expat pockets:

> In these rural areas in China, meth has become popular among populations not previously pegged as drug users. Truck drivers take it to stay awake for days on long-distance runs. Blue-collar or factory workers take it so they can work more hours, and to alleviate the tedium of mechanical drudgery. . . . The drug is also starting to penetrate urban areas as a party and sex accompaniment: it induces euphoria, and heightens sexual arousal and stamina.[24]

23. Jennifer Brea, "Beijing Police Round Up and Beat African Expats," *The Guardian*, September 25, 2007, www.guardian.co.uk/world/2007/sep/26/china.inter nationalcrime.

24. Eveline Chao, "Why 'Breaking Bad' Should Be Set in China," *Motherboard*, January 2, 2013, motherboard.vice.com/blog/why-breaking-bad-should-be-set-in -china.

杜冷丁

(**Demerol** / *Dùlěngdīng*) or pethidine is a painkiller that works like morphine by binding to receptors in the brain and inhibiting some of the signals associated with pain. It is often prescribed by doctors and used in hospital settings.

Why it is blocked: Even legal prescription drugs do not escape the censors. There doesn't seem to be a Demerol crisis in China, so it's perhaps just a precautionary block to prevent people from sharing information on finding and abusing Demerol. Demerol's most famous reported addict was Michael Jackson, who allegedly died from a cocktail of drugs that may have included Demerol.

迷奸

(literally, **dazed treachery** / *míjiān*) is better translated into English as "date rape," "drugged sex," or "**roofied**."

Why it is blocked: If sex is a sensitive topic, then forcible sex is even more so, since it carries the added dimension of criminality and injustice. Like in other countries around the world, in China the shame of being raped has caused some victims to commit suicide. In 2010, a police officer from Hunan drugged a sixteen-year-old girl before sexually assaulting her. After waking up, the girl jumped from the hotel room to her death. Internet commentators pilloried the fact that the man would likely not be executed because he was a policeman.[25]

25. Choi Chi-yuk, "Police Chief Sentenced for Causing Girl's Death," *South China Morning Post*, November 1, 2010, www.scmp.com/article/729129/police-chief
-sentenced-causing-girls-death.

射液

(inject / *shèyè*) literally means to shoot out liquid.

Why it is blocked: This is another word with two meanings, both of which are sensitive. The more clinical definition could be used to describe the injecting of drugs or even poisons (think Georgi Markov, the Bulgarian dissident, and his death after being pricked, while walking on the street, with a poison-tipped umbrella wielded by an assassin in 1978). However, the more common usage is to describe another kind of squirting: sexual ejaculation. Though it can be used to describe the act of male ejaculation, it is more commonly associated with female ejaculation or orgasm.

4

#people#

徐勤先

(**Xu Qinxian** / *Xú Qínxiān*) was a major general in the Chinese People's Liberation Army and the commander of the Thirty-Eighth Army during the 1989 Tiananmen crackdown. He famously refused an order to drive the students from the square when martial law was declared and was subsequently stripped of his command and jailed for five years.[1]

Why it is blocked: Xu's insubordination during the crackdown was not unique among soldiers, many of whom were sympathetic to the protesters' cause. However, his was the most prominent case, though it was not reported on within China for obvious reasons.

---

1. "六四抗命英雄徐勤先将军依然健在 (图)," 人民日报 (*People's Daily*), February 14, 2011, renminbao.com/rmb/articles/2011/2/14/54105.html.

蒋彦永

(**Jiang Yanyong** / *Jiǎng Yànyǒng*) is a Chinese physician who served as the chief physician of the 301[2] Military Hospital in Beijing during the severe acute respiratory syndrome (SARS) scandal in 2002–3.

Why it is blocked: Central authorities imposed a media blackout on SARS reporting after the first cases in late 2002. Jiang broke the government silence in April 2003 by e-mailing revelations about the severity of the crisis to the media, and the memo was subsequently leaked to *Time* magazine.[3] He followed this up the next year by writing a public letter to government officials that called for a reexamination of the 1989 Tiananmen crackdown and accusing the government of covering up the truth, after which he was detained by the state for over a month. He reentered the spotlight in 2009 when he submitted a letter to President Hu Jintao demanding an apology for his time spent under house arrest.[4]

---

2. 301 in Chinese characters (三〇一) is also blocked. However, "301" and "三零一" (with the alternative Chinese character for the digit 0) are unblocked.

3. Susan Jakes, "Beijing's SARS Attack," *Time*, April 8, 2003, www.time.com/time /world/article/0,8599,441615,00.html.

4. Emma Graham-Harrison, "China's SARS Hero Demands Apology for Detention," Reuters, March 12, 2009, www.reuters.com/article/2009/03/12/us-china-tiananmen -idUSTRE52B1F520090312?sp=true.

温云松

(**Wen Yunsong**, also known as **Winston Wen** / *Wēn Yúnsōng*) is a Chinese businessman and current CEO of Unihub Global Networks. He earned an MBA from the Kellogg School of Management at Northwestern University.

Why it is blocked: Wen is the son of current Chinese premier Wen Jiabao. As reported in the *Financial Times*, Wen Yunsong's name was blocked on search engines back in 2010, when his equity fund New Horizon Capital neared $1 billion in capital: "'The government and the younger Mr. Wen definitely don't want anyone in China to know that the premier's son is doing a big investment fund,' one person familiar with New Horizon said."[5]

Wen Jiabao's finances made headlines again in October 2012 when the *New York Times* ran a story about his family's immense wealth. Numerous individuals connected to the story were eventually blocked on Weibo, including Wen's mother, wife, younger brother, and brother-in-law.[6] As corruption is a major topic of contention among netizens and government employees alike, with innumerable officials such as Xi Jinping and Wen Jiabao promising to stamp out endemic political corruption, high-profile cases are often censored to prevent inflaming online anger.

---

5. Jamil Anderlini, "China Hush as Premier's Son Nears $1bn Target," *Financial Times*, January 26, 2010, www.ft.com/intl/cms/s/0/a1c487bc-0a97-11df-b35f-00144 feabdc0.html.

6. Jason Q. Ng, "Who in Wen Jiabao's Family Is Blocked on Weibo," *Blocked on Weibo*, November 4, 2012, blockedonweibo.tumblr.com/post/34995746840/who-in -wen-jiabaos-family-is-blocked-on-weibo.

刘宾雁

(**Liu Binyan** / *Liú Bīnyàn*) was a Chinese author and journalist.

Why it is blocked: He was labeled a rightist in 1957 for his writing, and even after his reputation was rehabilitated, he continued to critique the government throughout the ensuing decades. He is perhaps best known for *People or Monsters*, his 1979 book on Wang Shouxin, a government official who was involved in a corruption scandal. Liu was the president of the Chinese PEN Center (page 157) and served numerous stints in labor camps. He was known by many of his peers and readers as "China's conscience" (中国的良心).[7] Liu's searing reportage and commentary earned him a reputation as a government watchdog. He was finally expelled from the Chinese Communist Party after attempting to organize student demonstrations in December 1986, and he left for the United States in 1988. He died in 2005 while living in exile in the United States.

---

7. Others who have also held this unofficial honorific include the great Chinese writer Lu Xun.

彭丽媛

(Peng Liyuan / *Péng Lìyuán*) is a Chinese singer well known for her patriotic and rural folk songs during appearances on the annual state TV New Year's gala program. She is married to the current Chinese head of state, Xi Jinping, who took over as president of China and general secretary of the Communist Party in 2013.

Why it is blocked: Though Xi, like most high-level Communist Party officials, earns a block on Weibo, Peng is one of the few wives untarnished by scandal to receive that honor as well.[8] (Hu Jintao's wife is uncensored, though Wen Jiabao's wife is blocked because of corruption allegations; see page 92.) Peng's block is probably due to the combination of her being the incoming first lady and her already high profile as a glamorous celebrity. Like the model heroes in modern Chinese history, she is a member of the army (serving as a civilian with the rank of major general) who has had to sacrifice for her country—albeit in the form of lost commercial endorsement opportunities and the like.[9]

---

8. Zhou Enlai's wife, Deng Yingchao (邓颖超), through no "fault" of her own, is also blocked.

9. "'Being a soldier, Peng has lost many chances to sing commercially or appear in advertisements,' said one official report a few years ago, sympathetically recording that Peng 'felt a little bit lost' when watching other celebrities filming TV shows, advancing their careers. 'But when she thinks about the lovely soldiers, the soldiers who've been deeply touched by her songs, Peng knows that such glory and honor is irreplaceable.'" Melinda Liu, "China's Next First Lady Moves to a Bigger Stage," *Newsweek*, January 17, 2011, www.thedailybeast.com/newsweek/2011/01/18/china-s -next-first-lady-moves-to-a-bigger-stage.html.

方励之

(**Fang Lizhi** / *Fāng Lìzhī*) was a professor of astrophysics and board member and co-chair of Human Rights in China, an international NGO whose mission includes advancing the rule of law in China and generating pressure for social change in China. His writing inspired the pro-democracy student movement of 1986–87 and the Tiananmen Square protests of 1989. In June 1990, he was granted political asylum in the United States after much negotiating involving high-level diplomatic talks, a halfhearted confession of guilt,[10] and the promise of renewed financial assistance from Japan to China.[11] He died on April 7, 2012.

Why it is blocked: The *New York Times*'s obituary quotes Wang Dan, one of the student leaders of the 1989 Tiananmen protests, as saying, "Fang Lizhi has inspired the '89 generation and has awakened the people's yearning for human rights and democracy."[12]

10. Fang Lizhi, "My 'Confession,'" trans. Perry Link, *New York Review of Books*, June 23, 2011, www.nybooks.com/articles/archives/2011/jun/23/my-confession.

11. Akitoshi Miyashita, "Consensus or Compliance? *Gaiatsu*, Interests, and Japan's Foreign Aid," in *Japanese Foreign Policy in Asia and the Pacific: Domestic Interests, American Pressure, and Regional Integration*, ed. Akitoshi Miyashita and Yoichiro Sato (New York: Palgrave Macmillan, 2001), 44.

12. Michael Wines, "Fang Lizhi, Chinese Physicist and Seminal Dissident, Dies at 76," *New York Times*, April 7, 2012, www.nytimes.com/2012/04/08/world/asia/fang-lizhi-chinese-physicist-and-dissident-dies-at-76.html.

馬明心

(**Ma Mingxin** / *Mǎ Míngxīn*) was a Dungan Sufi master who was born in 1719. During the Qing Dynasty, he established the Jahriyya Sufi order in China, a school of Sufism—a sect of Islam—that was in opposition to the Khufiyya Sufis.

Why it is blocked: Jahriyya was considered to be a subversive religion in China, and after one of Ma's disciples, Su Sishisan (苏四十三), led an armed antigovernment uprising in 1781, Ma was arrested and beheaded.

刘荻

(**Liu Di** / *Liú Dí*) is a Chinese blogger and translator. She was awarded a Hellman-Hammett grant for writing by Human Rights Watch in 2007. According to Human Rights Watch, as of 2007, she was unemployed.

Why it is blocked: Her unemployment is not due to a lack of education—she graduated from Beijing Normal University with a psychology degree—but rather because she has been branded a dissident writer for online posts she made in 2002. Writing under the pseudonym 不锈钢老鼠 (Stainless Steel Rat, a character from Harry Harrison's science-fiction novels), she called for greater freedoms in China and once even jokingly discussed starting a political party where everyone could be chairman. She was later arrested for "being detrimental to state security" and jailed for one year even though she was never formally charged with a crime.[13] Her case became a cause célèbre for rights groups and her name was blocked on websites.[14] She was freed in 2003, but her name was still blocked on Weibo up until 2011.

---

13. Jim Yardley, "The Saturday Profile: A Chinese Bookworm Raises Her Voice in Cyberspace," *New York Times*, July 24, 2004, www.nytimes.com/2004/07/24/world/the-saturday-profile-a-chinese-bookworm-raises-her-voice-in-cyberspace.html.
14. James Borton, "A Blogger's Tale: The Stainless Steel Mouse," *Asia Times*, July 22, 2004, www.atimes.com/atimes/China/FG22Ad04.html.

吴仪

(Wu Yi / *Wú Yí*) was one of the vice premiers of the State Council of the People's Republic of China (see page 45) and the highest-ranking woman in Communist Party history. She graduated with a degree in petroleum engineering before the Cultural Revolution and worked her way up the political ladder, serving as vice mayor of Beijing from 1987 to 1991 and joining the Politburo in 2002 before retiring in 2008. In between she served as China's lead negotiator on numerous trade discussions, including China's ascension to the WTO, earning the nickname the "Iron Lady." Tough but well respected, she also successfully stepped in as health minister after the previous one was dismissed during the SARS crisis (see Jiang Yanyong, page 91). She was named *Forbes*'s second most powerful woman in the world in 2004, 2005, and 2007 (she was third in 2006).

Why it is blocked: Wu Yi was never mired in scandal like some of her colleagues, but Weibo blocks numerous politicians' names regardless of whether they've been tainted or not. The more prominent the politician, the more likely they'll be "protected" from online criticism. Most of the Politburo members are blocked, and all of the Standing Committee members were blocked as of October 2012. This changed markedly, however, after the Party Congress in November 2012, with many Politburo members being unblocked.[15]

---

15. As of January 13, 2013, only two of the twenty-five current Politburo members were still blocked: Liu Qibao and Li Zhanshu; of the retiring Seventeenth Politburo members, three were still blocked: Xu Caihou, Guo Boxiong, and Wen Jiabao. Though some have argued that the lack of blocks on certain politicians like Xi Jinping following the congress indicated that the government was opening up the Internet (Malcolm Moore, "Sina Weibo: China's Online Censors Relax Their

Liu Yandong is currently the highest-ranking female and one of only two women in the current twenty-five-member Politburo. The CCP has made efforts to recruit more women into the party, even instituting certain quotas for female cadres. Subsequently, the percentage of delegates to the bi-decade Party Congress has gradually crept up, with 23 percent of the 2012 delegates being women, up from 20 percent in 2007 and 18 percent in 2002.[16] However, women are still vastly underrepresented at higher levels, with less than 5 percent of the Central Committee being women and none in the most elite body, the Politburo Standing Committee.

Grip," *The Telegraph*, December 11, 2012, www.telegraph.co.uk/news/worldnews/asia/china/9736664/Sina-Weibo-Chinas-online-censors-relax-their-grip.html), in fact a search of websites that track deleted posts on Weibo would have showed that posts about Xi Jinping and other top leaders were still being deleted and that the search results being returned were highly filtered.

16. He Dan and Zhu Zhe, "Women Assume Bigger Role," *China Daily*, November 8, 2012, usa.chinadaily.com.cn/epaper/2012-11/08/content_15894798.htm.

丁先皇

(**Dinh Bo Linh** / *Dīng Xiānhuáng*) was the first emperor of Vietnam following the liberation of Vietnam after a millennium of Chinese control. He reigned from 968 until he was killed by a palace official in 979.

Why it is blocked: China has a complicated history with its former territories. Even today, you'll find Chinese folks who will claim (some jokingly, some seriously) that Korea, Vietnam, and other independent nations still rightfully belong to China. This sense of nationalism has erupted in land disputes in the East and South China Seas with these former territories and vassal states. However, why Dinh Bo Linh is singled out is curious.

冯正虎

(**Feng Zhenghu** / *Féng Zhènghǔ*) is a Chinese economist and a prominent defender of the rights of petitioners—the Chinese system for dealing with people with grievances. Citizens may submit a petition to their local designated petitioning bureau if they feel they have been wronged. If the situation is not resolved, they are then allowed to petition higher authorities, and, as a last resort, even permitted to travel to Beijing to present their case to the State Bureau for Letters and Visits if their grievance is not resolved in the lower bodies. Petitioners face hurdles at every level, and local officials have been known to hire thugs to intercept and detain petitioners who are known to be trying to appeal to higher levels—such appeals would be a black mark on the local officials' political records and inhibit their chances at promotion. Feng was jailed in 2001 for purported "illegal business activity" and served three years in prison.

Why it is blocked: Feng's audacious protest at Narita Airport, Tokyo, in 2009–10 brought him into the international spotlight. After traveling to Japan to receive medical treatment, he planned a return trip home to China in June 2009. However, he was refused entry back into the country. He tried a total of eight times in the following months, actually boarding four times, but was sent back by Chinese authorities to Japan each time. After the eighth time, in November, he protested his forced exile by refusing to leave the airport arrival zone. For the following three months, with the help of staff and strangers, he lived inside the airport, an act that the media likened to the Steven Spielberg movie *The Terminal*. He was finally allowed back into China in February 2010, but his continued work on behalf of petitioners led to his house arrest in February 2012.

李金

(**Kim Lee** / *Lǐ Jīn*) is the Chinese name of the American-born wife of Li Yang, the founder of Crazy English, a company that advocates learning English by shouting it as loudly as you can, usually in large groups, while performing hand motions.[17] They married in 2004 and have three daughters.

Why it is blocked: Li Yang's approach toward English-language learning has made him a lightning rod for both criticism and adoration throughout China. His lectures have been compared to Cultural Revolutionary–era rallies and cult meetings, and among his slogans is "Conquer English to Make China Stronger!"

His notoriety grew in 2011 when his wife, Kim Lee, accused him of domestic violence, posting images of bruises to her forehead, legs, and ear on Weibo. Li later admitted in interviews to slamming his wife to the floor, but claimed that it was "family business" and did not concern others. The drama continued when Lee posted screenshots of threatening text messages that Li had sent her. Lee filed for divorce in late 2011, and a Beijing court eventually granted her request in February 2013. During that time, Lee became a heroine to women in China and led a campaign to give domestic abuse victims greater rights and recognition in a country where the beating of wives often goes unprosecuted and socially unpunished.

---

17. Read: Evan Osnos, "Crazy English: The National Scramble to Learn a New Language Before the Olympics," *New Yorker*, April 28, 2008, www.newyorker.com /reporting/2008/04/28/080428fa_fact_osnos?currentPage=all. Watch: Film documentary by Zhang Yuan, *Crazy English*, 1999.

张筬雨

(**Zhang Xiaoyu** / *Zhāng Xiǎoyǔ*) is a Chinese model, arguably China's first famous nude model in the Internet age. Her name was among the most searched terms online in China in 2008.

Why it is blocked: Even though Zhang performed in only soft-core photography and videos, some of which might even fall into the art category, her work was still risqué enough to be considered unacceptable. In July 2010 the Ministry of Culture issued a notice that banned online game companies from using "vulgar marketing" after Zhang and other women known for their pretty faces, including Japanese pornographic film star Sora Aoi,[18] were hired to promote the games. Though Sora Aoi (蒼井空) is not blocked on Weibo and another Japanese adult video star, Ran Asakawa (武藤兰), was unblocked in early 2012, Zhang's name is still blocked, even though she announced on her blog in December 2009 that she was retiring from nude modeling.

---

18. Sora Aoi opened her Weibo account (www.weibo.com/u/1739928273) in November 2010 and gained 220,000 followers by the end of her first day. She writes in English, Chinese, and Japanese, and her posts range from the personal—pictures of her in a bathtub (tastefully covered by bubbles, of course)—to inspirational messages. Today, she has more than 13 million followers and is considered one of the most influential people on the service, though not enough to overcome the Chinese netizens' widespread anti-Japanese sentiment (see medicine patch flag, page 194) in 2012. On September 14 she posted a pair of images declaring friendship between China and Japan (www.weibo.com/1739928273/yBJYNt7Ol; www.weibo.com/1739928273/yBK5M4frh). The posts collected more than two hundred thousand comments, with commenters both supporting and vehemently attacking her.

文鲜明

(**Sun Myung Moon** / *Wén Xiānmíng*) was a Korean religious leader of the Holy Spirit Association for the Unification of World Christianity[19] (more commonly known as the Unification Church). The Unification Church claims to have several million members worldwide, derogatively called "Moonies" by critics. The church was most famous for the mass weddings it conducted in the 1980s. Moon died September 3, 2012.

Why it is blocked: Imprisoned by the North Korean government during the Korean War, Moon became stridently anti-Communist, making Communism's defeat a component of his religion. He encouraged the founding of the Confederation of the Associations for the Unification of the Societies of the Americas, an anti-Communist educational organization, and also was the founder and owner of the *Washington Times*, a conservative daily newspaper. In addition, critics described his church as cultlike and accused Moon of brainwashing adherents. China, with its wary view on religion (see Islam, page 190; Eastern Lightning, page 164; Milarepa, page 110; and Sacred Heart Cathedral, page 204), no doubt considered Moon and his ideology dangerous.

---

19. 世界基督教统一神灵协会, the full Chinese name for the religion, is one of the longest unique phrases blocked on Weibo.

王文怡

(**Wang Wenyi** / *Wáng Wényí*) is a reporter for the *Epoch Times* (see leave a political party, page 127). She holds a PhD in pharmacology from the University of Chicago and is a Falun Gong practitioner.

Why it is blocked: In 2001, Wang verbally accosted former president Jiang Zemin while he was touring the island of Malta, telling him to stop killing Falun Gong members. In April 2006, she obtained press credentials to report on Hu Jintao's official visit to the White House. As Hu presented a speech, she stood up, unfurled a banner, and yelled at him and President George W. Bush, who was sitting beside him, for several minutes before Secret Service agents detained her. Her disturbance was widely reported in Western media, with some describing it as a protest against China's reported organ harvesting from Falun Gong members (see Sujiatun, page 132) and others as rude heckling. After the incident, she resigned from the *Epoch Times*.[20] She was initially charged with disorderly conduct, but the charges were dropped two months later.

---

20. The *Epoch Times* writes in an addendum to a 2011 editorial by Wang, "The *Epoch Times* did not have advance notice of the protest and would not have approved of it if asked." Wang Wenyi, "Why I Protested Hu Jintao at the White House," *Epoch Times*, January 17, 2011, www.theepochtimes.com/n2/opinion/wenyi-wang-why-i-protested -hu-jintao-at-the-white-house-49520.html.

费孝通

(**Fei Xiaotong**[21] / *Fèi Xiàotōng*) was one of China's most noted social scientists. A popular intellectual in China, he was also equally celebrated outside, with his *Peasant Life in China: A Field Study of Country Life in the Yangtze Valley* commonly assigned in Western anthropology and sociology classes. As an intellectual who supported Western approaches to studying Chinese culture, he suffered greatly during the Anti-Rightist Movement in the 1950s and the Cultural Revolution in the 1960s. He was politically rehabilitated in the 1970s, after which he wrote prolifically and became a ubiquitous presence on Chinese television. He died in 2005 at the age of ninety-four.

Why it is blocked: After being rehabilitated, Fei led a mostly noncontroversial life, making this block seem a bit odd. Perhaps it has to do with his negative relationship to the Cultural Revolution or his support of common people, workers, and industrial development in the countryside.

21. His name is also commonly translated into English as Hsiao Tung Fei, a relic of the days when the Wade-Giles system was the most popular transliteration method to Romanize Chinese names into English.

雷洁琼

(**Lei Jieqiong** / *Léi Jiéqióng*) was a founder and former chair of the China Association for Promoting Democracy (CAPD), one of the eight officially sanctioned non-Communist political parties in China. She was a noted legal scholar and sociologist, having studied in the United States and graduated with a master's degree in sociology from the University of Southern California. She was also a strong advocate for women—supporting reforms, training women, and writing about working women.[22] She is also esteemed for her efforts to bring sociology back into Peking University's curriculum.[23] Lei died in 2011 at the age of 106. Her funeral was attended by top leaders from the Communist Party, including Hu Jintao, Wen Jiabao, Wu Bangguo, Li Keqiang, and Xi Jinping.

Why it is blocked: Though it may appear quite progressive for the Communist Party to allow political groups like the CAPD and the KMT to exist, the Party has effectively neutered them, and their continued existence is mostly a token effort at being a multiparty state. Though Lei is well respected,[24] especially for her work during the Japanese invasion of China, she and the CAPD have been

---

22. Lily Xiao Hong Lee and Clara Wing-chung Ho, *Biographical Dictionary of Chinese Women*, vol. 2, (Armonk, NY: M.E. Sharpe, 2003), 294.

23. Yu Lintao, "Dedicated to Education: Chinese Social Work Pioneer Dies at 106," *Beijing Review*, January 27, 2011, www.bjreview.com.cn/life/txt/2011-01/23/content_327939.htm.

24. USC president C.L. Max Nikias said of Lei: "A devoted teacher and an internationally renowned scholar whose academic work spanned law, sociology, demography and family dynamics, she also was extraordinarily dedicated to her country, achieving prominence as a political leader on the world stage" (news.usc.edu/#!/article/30156/In-Memoriam-Lei-Jieqiong-106).

politically co-opted. In a 2007 speech, Li Keqiang praised the CAPD's role in the CCP-led "multiparty cooperation," and Lei was hailed by Jia Qinglin, a top Party official, as "a sincere friend of the CPC."[25] Lei appears to be a noncontroversial figure, but her potential as a vehicle for criticism of China's one-party state may be the cause for her block.

25. Annette Moore, "In Memoriam: Lei Jieqiong, 106," *University of Southern California News*, January 14, 2011, www.china.org.cn/english/China/234093.htm.

黎智英

(**Jimmy Lai** / *Lí Zhìyīng*) is a Hong Kong entrepreneur. He was born in Guangzhou in southern China before escaping to Hong Kong at age twelve. His rags-to-riches story began with him working as a child laborer at a garment factory. In 1981, he founded the Hong Kong–based clothing retailer Giordano. In 2009, *Forbes* estimated his net worth at $660 million.

Why it is blocked: It is not his entrepreneurial spirit that causes Jimmy Lai to be blocked. After the Tiananmen incident in 1989, Lai started the tabloid *Next* magazine,[26] which combined sensational entertainment fodder with hard-hitting news reporting. In 1995, he started *Apple Daily*, which prominently criticized the Communist Party and pro-China government officials in Hong Kong. He has been called Hong Kong's Rupert Murdoch, and his empire's newspapers and magazines in Taiwan and Hong Kong are among the most read in each (though his TV stations are less successful).

His publications are banned in China, and mainland officials banned his autobiography, *I Am Jimmy Lai*, in 2011, shutting down the mainland publisher, Zhuhai Publishing House, that dared publish it. Lai was also the source of controversy in 2011 when it was reported that he had donated millions to Hong Kong's Civic Party and Democratic Party, in effect funding opposition to the pro–mainland China ruling party.

---

26. *Next* might be most familiar to Americans for one of its sister groups, the Taiwan-based Next Media Animation (NMA), which is a subsidiary of their parent company, Next Media. NMA is best known for producing a series of humorous computer graphic animations of news stories, including ones about Tiger Woods's car crash in 2009 and the Jet Blue flight attendant incident in 2010.

密勒日巴

(**Milarepa** / *Mìlèrìbā*) is one of Tibet's most famous yogis and po-
ets. He was born in the eleventh century, and he was said to have
studied and performed dark sorcery during his youth, deeds that he
regretted later in life. He eventually revised his ways and studied
under the Tibetan Buddhist teacher Marpa the Translator, and after twelve years achieved total enlightenment, purportedly the first
person to do so in just one lifetime. In statues and representations,
he is often depicted with a hand raised to his ear, which some claim
to be a symbol of his receptivity to Tantric teachings or learning
through song.

Why it is blocked: Religion is sensitive in China, and Milarepa's
Tibetan roots may enhance this, but 密勒日巴 still seems an unlikely target to be blocked. Buddhism is an officially recognized religion in China, and Milarepa's teachings seem quite innocent and
haven't been "hijacked" by cults. Perhaps it has something to do
with his connection to black magic—otherwise the reason seems
obscure.

阿沛·阿旺晋美

(**Ngapoi Ngawang Jigme** / *Āpèi Āwàng Jìnměi*), also known as just Ngabo, was a Tibetan aristocrat with a long career in public service. His roles ranged from fighting the Communist army as governor general of the Tibetan armed forces in Chamdo to later serving as a Tibetan representative to the Chinese National People's Congress from 1954 to 1988. He was also the first president of Tibet after it was classified as an autonomous region in 1965 (see West Ujimqin, page 22, note 23) and a key adviser to the fourteenth Dalai Lama. He died in December 2009, and his passing was mourned by Chinese officials and state media.

Why it is blocked: Ngabo was the chief delegate sent by the fourteenth Dalai Lama to Beijing in May 1951 to negotiate a peace settlement for Tibet after China defeated the Tibetan army the previous year. However, Ngabo and the Tibetan delegation were pressured to accept a seventeen-point agreement that officially handed sovereignty of Tibet over to China. The Dalai Lama later repudiated the agreement, but China has refused all efforts to cancel or alter it, and has affirmed that the treaty is legitimate.

Ngabo has been labeled a traitor to Tibet for his role in the seventeen-point agreement and for his collaboration with the Chinese government in the decades after. According to the *South China Morning Post*, he had not been back to visit Tibet from 1991 until his death.[27] Though the fourteenth Dalai Lama later recognized the extraordinarily difficult position Ngabo had been put in and asserted that Ngabo "had done his best" and that he "always had complete

27. "Tibetan Political Survivor Dies Weeks Before 100th Birthday," *South China Morning Post*, December 24, 2009, www.scmp.com/article/702065/tibetan-political -survivor-dies-weeks-100th-birthday.

trust in [Ngabo],"[28] others bemoan how Ngabo did not do more to protect and save the tenth Panchen Lama, who was sentenced to sixteen years in prison for criticizing the government's treatment of Tibetans. Defenders say Ngabo did genuinely try to uphold Tibetan values and autonomy by working from the inside to effect change.

28. "Transcript of Video-Conference with His Holiness the Dalai Lama and Chinese Activists," Office of the Holiness of the Dalai Lama, January 20, 2011, www.dalai lama.com/news/post/641-transcript-of-video-conference-with-his-holiness-the-dalai -lama-and-chinese-activists.

5

#scandals# #disasters# #rumors#

倒台事件

(literally, **downfall incident** / *dàotái shìjiàn*) is most often used to describe a politician's purge from the government after a scandal.

Why it is blocked: A fall from power denotes a failure on the part not only of the politician, but also of the Communist Party, since it is the Party that essentially appoints all key government officials. Thus, scandals, purges, and mentions of downfalls are often scrubbed clean online. In 2012, the most visible fall from power[1] was Bo Xilai's ouster (see page 118). However, in a new development, Bo's name was unblocked in September 2012, just after he was formally expelled from the Communist Party, indicating that Bo was to be made a scapegoat.

---

1. Though certainly not the first in CCP history. See Chen Xitong (page 119) and Zhao Ziyang (page 59, note 43) or read more about the mysterious Lin Biao plane crash, among many others.

万武义

(**Wan Wuyi** / *Wàn Wǔyì*) is the director of domestic news at Xinhua, the state news agency.

Why it is blocked: Though a number of Communist Party leaders and politicians are blocked on Weibo, it may seem odd for a common bureaucrat—albeit a high-level one—to merit the same treatment. However, Wan made headlines in 2010 when the British newspaper the *Telegraph* reported that he had possibly defected during a training trip in the United Kingdom.[2] Though Wan immediately came out publicly and dispelled the rumors, claiming that back pain had delayed his return trip home, commenters had a field day with the story.

2. Malcolm Moore, "China's Government News Chief 'Missing' in Britain," *The Telegraph*, July 27, 2010, www.telegraph.co.uk/news/worldnews/asia/china/7913013 /Chinas-government-news-chief-missing-in-Britain.html.

七五八大洪水

(the **Great Flood of August 1975** / *Qīwŭ Bā Dàhóngshuĭ*) refers to the massive rainfall and subsequent flooding that took place in Henan Province in 七五八 (literally, seven five eight).[3]

Why it is blocked: During that event, the Banqiao Dam collapsed, with estimates of 90,000–230,000 people dying. Reports are that poor construction and a record rainfall were to blame. However, files about the incident have already been declassified, so it's curious that this thirty-eight-year-old event is still blocked.

---

3. Chinese historians and people regularly refer to significant dates in Chinese history in some combination of month, date, and year (not that much different from how Americans refer to the terrorist attacks in 2001 as "9/11"). The most famous of these number-date phrases of course is 六四 (six four, or June 4, the date of the Tiananmen Square crackdown in 1989).

讣告

(**obituary** / *fùgào*) is a news article that announces the death of a person and that can provide an account of the person's life and information about the upcoming funeral.

Why it is blocked: If one had to guess, blocking this term may be an attempt to prevent false rumors of deaths from spreading. Weibo employs a rumor-control team whose purpose is to snuff out such falsehoods.[4] The team was likely very busy back in February 2011, when rumors spread that Kim Jong-un, the new head of North Korea, had been assassinated. Similarly, former Chinese president Jiang Zemin's supposed demise also gained traction on Weibo back in July 2011 before all such news was censored. As of today, both Kim Jong-un and Jiang Zemin are assumed still to be alive.

---

4. Jon Russell, "Sina Weibo 'Rumor Control' Team Explains How It Keeps the Web 'Unpolluted,'" *Next Web*, November 9, 2011, thenextweb.com/asia/2011/11/09/sina -weibo-rumor-control-team-explains-how-it-keeps-the-web-unpolluted.

薄熙来

(**Bo Xilai** / *Bó Xīlái*) was the Party secretary of Chongqing from 2007 to 2012. He was the son of Bo Yibo, one of the Eight Elders (see page 6) and a prominent Chinese Communist Party official. Bo Xilai was speculated to be a prime candidate for appointment to the highest governing body in China, the Politburo Standing Committee, until he was ousted from office in March 2012 and officially expelled from the Communist Party in September 2012.

Why it is blocked: This is a case where what is *not blocked* is more interesting than what is. Bo Xilai was involved in a major controversy when his police chief visited the American consulate in a nearby city, supposedly in a bid to request political asylum in exchange for offering to reveal to authorities his boss's corruption and Bo's wife's murder of a British citizen. Under normal circumstances, one would assume a nervous Internet company would play it safe and block everything associated with the incident, and for a time, the police chief's name, 王立军 (Wang Lijun), was blocked, as was Bo Xilai's. However, both were subsequently unblocked, and Bo Xilai's name even became a trending topic on Weibo after his removal was announced in early March. Speculation is that the Chinese leadership ordered Weibo to unblock Bo's name in order openly to purge him and the cloud hanging over him before the transition to new leadership later this year. Bo Xilai was reblocked on March 17, 2012, and existing posts were selectively pruned. Bo was finally unblocked for good when he was kicked out of the Party in September 2012.

陈希同

(**Chen Xitong** / *Chén Xītóng*) was the Party secretary of Beijing from 1992 to 1995 and mayor from 1983 to 1993, during which time he notably asserted that only two hundred people had died during the Tiananmen crackdown.[5] He was dismissed on corruption charges in 1995 and was imprisoned for eight years before being released on medical parole.

Why it is blocked: The parallels between Chen's downfall and Bo Xilai's (see page 118) are quite interesting. Both were rising stars within the CCP Politburo and leaders of prominent cities. Both were arguably undone by a mixture of arrogance (Bo for "trying to rally public opinion in favor of his now-defunct bid to join the Politburo Standing Committee"[6]; Chen for "boasting that his power was beyond anyone's reach"[7]) and corruption (although Chen's was demonstrably much less than was initially reported in the mid-nineties; in the end, he personally took something in the neighborhood of $100,000 in bribes, most in the form of gifts[8]—small potatoes, considering what others in China have gotten away with). Personal and political reasons were also involved. Each man's deputy mayor also played a sensational role in his fall: Wang Lijun

---

5. Daniel Southerland, "Mayor Revises Tiananmen Toll to 200 Civilians," *Houston Chronicle*, July 1, 1989, www.chron.com/CDA/archives/archive.mpl/1989_634246 /mayor-revises-tiananmen-toll-to-200-civilians.html.

6. A. McLaren, "A Shot Across the Bo," *Foreign Policy*, March 15, 2012, www .foreignpolicy.com/articles/2012/03/15/a_shot_across_the_bo.

7. Seth Faison, "Ex–Party Chief in Beijing Gets 16 Years in Prison," *New York Times*, July 31, 1998, www.nytimes.com/1998/07/31/world/ex-party-chief-in-beijing-gets-16 -years-in-prison.html.

8. Wu Zhong, "A Fight Against Rot at the Core," *Asia Times*, April 17, 2008, www .atimes.com/atimes/China/JD17Ad02.html.

sparked Bo's purge with his visit to the American consulate in Chengdu, while Wang Baosen committed suicide under suspicious circumstances. Chen's son was sentenced to prison as well; Bo's merely has to suffer the infamy of being known as not owning a Ferrari.[9]

Furthermore, the Communist Party pulled out all the stops to smear Chen, including branding him as "corrupt and decadent." Newspapers intimated that he had a taste for "entertaining young female television presenters,"[10] and it later came out that he cavorted about with a mistress who was fifteen years old. A thinly veiled roman à clef about Chen titled *The Wrath of Heaven* was released, then quickly banned, in 1997. This formula for branding an ousted leader as a sexually immoral person was repeated when Bo Xilai was kicked out of the Party in October 2012. Among the charges listed against Bo was the revelation that he had numerous mistresses.

9. Jeremy Page, "China's Red Star Denies Son Drives a Red Ferrari," China Real Time Report, *Wall Street Journal* blog, March 9, 2012, blogs.wsj.com/chinarealtime /2012/03/09/china-red-star-denies-son-drives-a-red-ferrari. (See also Crown Prince Party, page 18, note 19.)

10. Seth Faison, "Ex–Party Chief in Beijing Gets 16 Years in Prison," *New York Times*, July 31, 1998, www.nytimes.com/1998/07/31/world/ex-party-chief-in-beijing -gets-16-years-in-prison.html.

我的奋斗

(**Mein Kampf** / *Wǒde Fèndòu*) is an autobiography and a book of political theory by Adolf Hitler.

Why it is blocked: As in Germany and a number of other countries, the sale of *Mein Kampf* is restricted in China. In fact, merely searching for the title on Amazon China or Taobao, a Chinese shopping website, from the United States will cut off your Internet connection to the site (curiously, Chinese users can search without hassle). Besides being the work of one of the twentieth century's most infamous dictators, *Mein Kampf* is also known for its inflammatory anti-Communist views—another reason for the CCP to ban it. However, due to his strong leadership and emphasis on social stability, Hitler is reportedly admired by some Chinese—though this is arguably due to ignorance rather than actual malice (the same way some Westerners naively venerate Mao without being aware of his disastrous policies during the Cultural Revolution). In May 2011, there was a bizarre Internet rumor that Hitler was raised by a Chinese family in Vienna, with a number of bloggers taking pride in China's supposed connection with Hitler.[11]

阿道夫·希特勒 (Adolf Hitler / *ādàofū xītèlè*) is not blocked on Weibo, Amazon.cn, or Taobao.

---

11. Richard Komaiko, "Hitler and the Chinese Internet Generation," *Asia Times*, May 25, 2011, www.atimes.com/atimes/China/ME25Ad01.html.

上蔡县

(**Shangcai** / *Shàngcài xiàn*) is a county in Henan Province and part of Zhumadian City. Zhumadian is home to sixty-two different dams, including Banqiao Dam (see the Great Flood of August 1975, page 116). Shangcai contains a number of villages, including Wenlou (文楼村).

Why it is blocked: A densely populated farming community, Shangcai remained quite impoverished until the arrival of blood plasma buyers in the 1990s provided a modicum of wealth for the poor farmers, who made roughly $5 each time they gave blood— enough for some to build houses one beam at a time and afford to send their children to school. However, due to an appalling lack of sterilization and safety standards, nearly seven hundred in the town of three thousand have become infected by HIV over the years.

The case of the "AIDS village" (as Wenlou came to be called) tarnished just about everyone: health officials for not regulating the blood drives until 1996; blood profiteers for cutting corners on equipment and sanitary practices; local officials for receiving kickbacks when welcoming in the incompetent blood takers; surrounding communities for shunning the village after rumors spread of a mysterious sickness; central and provincial authorities for trying to sweep the scandal under the rug—ignoring reports from doctors that AIDS was sweeping through the village—and leaving the village to fend for itself;[12] local officials again for siphoning

---

12. To the government's credit, a gleaming new AIDS treatment facility has since been erected, and orphanages have been established to care for the hundreds of children who have lost their parents to AIDS. Wen Jiabao visited Wenlou in 2005 and 2007, visits that, according to some, were as much political theater as they were genuine expressions of caring. "The Premier's Visit to China's Most Infamous AIDS

away most of the aid[13] that came in once the story broke globally in 2001;[14] and the state media for playing along with the Party and holding up Wenlou as a model village that overcame adversity and is now on the path to recovery.[15] The only heroes of this tragedy besides the courageous victims in Wenlou and their steadfast families are the two doctors who traveled to Wenlou during the crisis, treating the patients and publicizing their plight: Gui Xi'en and Gao Yaojie.

Village," *Black and White Cat*, December 3, 2007, www.blackandwhitecat.org/2007/12/03/the-premiers-visit-to-chinas-most-infamous-aids-village.

13. *Asia Weekly* (亞洲週刊) has a devastating story on the malfeasance by Wenlou's Party secretary, Liu Yuemei. Translated by Roland Soong, "Impeaching Corrupt Officials in Henan AIDS Villages," *EastSouthWestNorth*, January 5, 2006, www.zona europa.com/20060105_1.htm.

14. Adam Brookes, "Bad Blood Spreads Aids in China," BBC, May 30, 2001, news.bbc.co.uk/2/hi/asia-pacific/1359670.stm.

15. An English article in the *People's Daily*, the state newspaper, contains the following section headings: "Death Rate Approaches a Normal Level"; "AIDS-Hit Women Give Birth to Healthy Babies"; " 'Sunshine Home' Set Up in Every Town"; and "AIDS Patient Families Rekindle Hopes of Life." "China's 'AIDS Village' Steps Out of Shadow," *People's Daily*, China.org.cn, November 10, 2005, www.china.org.cn/english/China/148320.htm. An "inspirational" romance film, *Love for Life* (最爱), about an AIDS village and featuring stars Zhang Ziyi and Aaron Kwok, showed in Chinese theaters in 2011. The movie was supported by the government.

非正常死亡

(**unnatural death** / *fēizhèngcháng sǐwáng*) refers to the end of one's life by anything but natural health causes, including accidents (drowning, traffic, fire), intentional acts (murder, suicide, state executions), and negligence (medical malpractice).

Why it is blocked: Besides its potential to call attention to deaths caused by police and security, 非正常死亡 can also be used to refer to two sensitive historical periods: the "Three Years of Difficult Period" (三年困难时期, the official Party euphemism for the Great Famine of 1958–61) and the Cultural Revolution. Estimates are that tens of millions of people died due to government ignorance, neglect, and persecution during these two events.

富女

(**rich woman** / *fù nǚ*) is a term for a woman with money. It may refer to one who is independently wealthy due to her job, but more typically it is used derogatorily online to criticize the obscene wealth of the wives, mistresses, and daughters of rich businessmen and government officials.

Why it is blocked: The term is blocked because of a June 2011 incident involving a 富女. Twenty-year-old Guo Meimei (郭美美), who listed her job title as commercial general manager of the "China Red Cross Chamber of Commerce," had been posting for months about her glamorous lifestyle on Weibo, which included photos of her horseback riding, flying in first class, and flaunting her prized possessions: Hermès handbags, an orange Lamborghini, and a white Maserati luxury car. When Internet users discovered her account, investigations and outrage spread throughout Weibo. Eventually, netizens identified Wang Jun, a board member at a company who organized charity drives for the official Red Cross Society of China, as perhaps being Guo's boyfriend, and he subsequently resigned from his job.[16] Chinese Red Cross officials denied

---

16. Though some news reports claimed that the luxury cars were actually Wang's, Guo claimed in a TV interview that Wang had gifted them to her. Further confusion was sown when Guo and her mother claimed that Wang Jun was merely a close family friend and Guo's "godfather" (George Ding, "Guo Meimei Responds to Red Cross Controversy—Part 1," *chinaSMACK*, August 13, 2011, www.chinasmack.com/2011 /videos/guo-meimei-responds-to-red-cross-controversy-lang-xianping-interview -part-1.html), a line that state-aligned media like the *Global Times* pushed (Xuyang Jingjing, "Guo Meimei Reaches for the Stars While the Red Cross Sinks," *Global Times*, September 16, 2011, www.globaltimes.cn/NEWS/tabid/99/ID/675618/Guo -Meimei-reaches-for-the-stars-while-the-Red-Cross-sinks.aspx).

any connection with Guo, though they admitted her supposed organization did exist. Netizens demanded a full accounting of where their donations had gone, and the Chinese Red Cross launched an investigation, which turned up improprieties. However, despite the thorough investigation, the Chinese Red Cross's reputation was already seriously damaged, and donations fell by nearly 60 percent in 2011 compared to the previous year.[17]

The Chinese Red Cross scandal was just one of a series that shook Chinese confidence in charities—which are supposed to be tightly regulated by the government. One of the most notorious occurred in the pre–social media age: in 2001, reporters uncovered vast corruption in the China Youth Development Foundation (CYDF) program Project Hope, which aimed to help impoverished children get an education.[18] In August 2011, another rich female was ensnared in a charity scandal: twenty-four-year-old Lu Xingyu (卢星宇), the daughter of billionaire Lu Junqin (卢俊卿), was accused of extracting exorbitant management fees of over $20 million from her charity China-Africa Project Hope, another CYDF-affiliated program. Her rambling defense of the charity was lambasted by netizens.[19] And on an individual level, Zhang Ziyi was accused of charity fraud and of not fulfilling donations as promised in 2010. In an interview she tearfully admitted to an oversight on her part and donated the balance of what she had pledged.[20]

---

17. Though this may be due partly to the fact that fewer natural disasters than usual occurred in 2011, the Guo Meimei scandal and the subsequent loss of credibility was undoubtedly a major reason as well. "Donations to China Red Cross Drop 59 pct in 2011: Report," Xinhua, June 28, 2012, news.xinhuanet.com/english/china/2012-06/28/c_131682138.htm.

18. David Bandurski, "Chinese Authorities Intensify Pressure on Veteran Journalist Zhai Minglei," China Media Project, November 30, 2007, cmp.hku.hk/2007/11/30/752.

19. Fauna, "'Lu Meimei' & China-Africa Project Hope Controversy," *chinaSMACK*, August 22, 2011, www.chinasmack.com/2011/stories/lu-meimei-china-africa-project-hope-charity-controversy.html.

20. Raymond Zhou, "Actress Denies Charity Fraud," *China Daily*, March 16, 2010, www.chinadaily.com.cn/china/2010-03/16/content_9593921.htm.

退党

(**leave a political party** / *tuìdǎng*), in this case, the Communist Party.

Why it is blocked: In most contexts, 退党 does not refer to the forced expulsions of Communist Party members after a scandal, but instead refers to an equally vexing problem for the government: people voluntarily electing to quit and resign from the Party. Roughly 80 million people are official Chinese Communist Party members, making it the largest political party in the world. However, one does not simply sign up—members must apply[21] and are chosen from a pool of applicants: government statistics report that some 20 million apply annually, and in the end only 14 percent are accepted. Joining the club comes with a number of perks, including the potential for better career opportunities.[22]

Thus, renouncing one's membership is a rather big deal, and some news outlets have been keeping careful track of those who publicly do so.[23] "Tuidang" became a movement in 2004 after the

---

21. The Party has sought to encourage young people to join, even utilizing hilariously dated music videos extolling the Party: Sinostand, "Applying to Join the Chinese Communist Party—Music Video (w/ English subtitles)," YouTube, March 30, 2012, www.youtube.com/watch?v=Ei6fRQoov60&feature=player_embedded#!.

22. "Guest Post—Why I Didn't Join the Communist Party," *Seeing Red in China*, January 18, 2011, seeingredinchina.com/2011/01/18/guest-post-why-i-didnt-join-the-communist-party.

23. Not coincidentally, most of these reports come from the *Epoch Times* and New Tang Dynasty Television, both of which are media outlets financed by the supporters of the Falun Gong (see Sujiatun, page 132), the persecuted religious sect in China. Though the *Epoch Times* and NTD both perform valuable reporting, the stories chosen and the coverage provided on mainland Chinese issues are heavily biased against the Communist Party and thus should be viewed skeptically.

Chinese-language newspaper the *Epoch Times* published a collection of nine editorials criticizing the Communist Party. The Global Service Center for Quitting the Chinese Communist Party (GSCQCCP), based in Flushing, New York, claims that an extraordinary 100 million people and counting have already quit (highly unlikely considering there are only 80 million in the Party today) and has set up a website[24] to assist those who wish to withdraw from the Party. This group, and organized quitting marches in American cities and Hong Kong, have turned "tuidang" into a sensitive word. The GSCQCCP and the *Epoch Times* are closely allied, if not explicitly connected.[25]

---

24. Global Service Center for Quitting the Chinese Communist Party, accessed December 17, 2012, www.quitccp.org.

25. The sheer amount of coverage, and the number of mentions of the GSCQCCP in the *Epoch Times* are overwhelming. As of October 2012, 105 news articles in the *Epoch Times*'s archive had mentioned "the Global Service Center for Quitting the Chinese Communist Party." The two websites also share similar rhetoric and even the same colors.

宋祖英

(**Song Zuying** / *Sòng Zǔyīng*) is arguably the most famous soprano singer in China. Born in Hunan, she is of Miao ethnicity. She studied music and dancing in college before joining the Chinese People's Liberation Army Naval Song and Dance Troupe. Like fellow Chinese singer Peng Liyuan (see page 94), she is a noted patriot, holding an officer's rank in the Chinese navy. She has sung at numerous state functions, including the Chinese New Year's gala and with Plácido Domingo during the closing ceremonies of the 2008 Beijing Olympics.

Why it is blocked: Song reportedly had a long-running affair with former president Jiang Zemin, who was forty years her senior, and allegedly owed much of her career to him.[26] Jiang was neither the first nor the last supreme leader of China rumored to be sleeping with much younger women. A 1999 American diplomatic cable published by WikiLeaks relayed rumors that Hu Jintao, while serving as vice president, had engaged in an affair with a twenty-something TV host who was younger than his own daughter. And it has been well documented that Mao Zedong enjoyed the ministrations of numerous young women, openly indulging in mistresses.

26. Mark Oneill, "A Corruption Trail Leads to Jiang Zemin," *Asia Sentinel*, March 7, 2007, www.asiasentinel.com/index.php?option=com_content&task=view&id=409 &Itemid=31.

锦州监狱

(**Jinzhou Prison** / *Jǐnzhōu Jiānyù*), located in Liaoning Province, held more than 1,500 inmates in the 1980s. It is one of China's *laogai* (劳改), the "reform through labor" camps.[27] In *laogai*, prisoners are forced to work, with most either performing agricultural work or manufacturing products for sale. Like other *laogai*, Jinzhou Prison has, in addition to its internal administrative name, public "enterprise names": the Jinzhou Switch Factory and the Jinzhou Jinkai Electrical Group. According to the Laogai Research Foundation,[28] the prison is not merely self-sufficient due to its sales of high-voltage switch cabinets and other electrical equipment; it actually turns a substantial profit of nearly $10 million annually and was named one of the ten best enterprises in China in 2006.[29]

---

27. Not to be confused with *laojiao* (劳教) or "reeducation through labor" camps. Those sent to *laogai* have been officially sentenced by the court system, while *laojiao* are black jails of sorts, where petty criminals, drug users, and dissidents alike can be detained outside of the legal system for up to eighteen months without trial. According to reports, anywhere from 200,000 to more than 1 million people are housed in these detention centers. Both *laojiao* and *laogai* have been criticized for their lack of transparency and forced penal labor. For a summary of the system read: Jim Yardley, "Issue in China: Many in Jails Without Trial," *New York Times*, May 9, 2005, www.nytimes.com/2005/05/09/international/asia/09china.html.

28. The Laogai Research Foundation was founded by Harry Wu, an activist who was imprisoned for nineteen years in China and forced to work in factories, mines, and fields. It publishes an annual handbook documenting every known work prison in China and runs a museum in Washington, DC, that promotes awareness of *laogai*.

29. Laogai Research Foundation, *Laogai Handbook: 2007–2008* (Washington, DC: Laogai Research Foundation, 2008), laogai.org/system/files/u1/handbook2008-all.pdf.

Why it is blocked: *Laogai,* regardless of their financial success, aren't typically blocked on Weibo. Other notable *laogai,* such as Qincheng Prison in Beijing, which has housed many Tiananmen Square protesters and other political dissidents, is unblocked. Jinzhou is sensitive because of a very particular prisoner detained there: political dissident Liu Xiaobo (see charter, page 141). He was transferred there from Beijing in May 2010. A little more than four months later, he was awarded the Nobel Peace Prize (see empty stool, page 145). However, due to a medical condition, he will not likely be forced to work and will reportedly spend most of his time in solitary confinement—probably a preferred outcome for officials who might be nervous that he'll spread his subversive ideas.[30]

---

30. Megan Fluker, "Liu Xiaobo Transferred to Jinzhou Prison, Liaoning Province," *Laogai Blog,* June 14, 2010, laogai.org/blog/liu-xiaobo-transferred-jinzhou-prison -liaoning-province.

苏家屯

(**Sujiatun** / *Sūjiātún*) is a district in Shenyang, one of China's largest cities. Sujiatun is known mostly for its agriculture, its industry, and the Sujiatun Thrombosis Hospital.

Why it is blocked: The Sujiatun Thrombosis Hospital is a public hospital that opened in 1988. It has gained recognition for its advanced medical research and notoriety for an accusation by the *Epoch Times* in March 2006 that the hospital had been harvesting organs from detained Falun Gong members. At the request of a Falun Gong advocacy group, Canadian MP David Kilgour and human rights lawyer David Matas issued a report in July 2006 that confirmed Chinese authorities had put to death a "large but unknown number of Falun Gong prisoners of conscience" and taken their organs to service a growing demand for transplants. Independent observers were concerned by the lack of hard evidence or confirmed eyewitness accounts in the report, which consisted of only circumstantial evidence. Follow-up investigations, including ones by human rights activist Harry Wu[31] and the U.S. State Department,[32] failed to uncover signs of forced organ harvesting of Falun Gong members at Sujiatun. Though it is impossible to rule out that organ harvesting may have taken place in the past, reports of an intentional government program to do so are currently unfounded.

31. Roland Soong, "Wu Hongda's Statement on the Sujiatun Concentration Camp," *EastSouthWestNorth*, August 6, 2006, www.zonaeuropa.com/20060806_1.htm. See also Jinzhou Prison (page 130, note 28) for more on Harry Wu.

32. "U.S. Finds No Evidence of Alleged Concentration Camp in China," IIP Digital, U.S. Department of State, April 16, 2006, iipdigital.usembassy.gov/st/english/text trans/2006/04/20060416141157uhyggep0.5443231.html#axzz29Ie2AiIN.

6

#information# #media#

开 放 杂 志

(**Open Magazine** / *kāifàng zázhì*) is a monthly Hong Kong magazine founded in January 1987. Its original title was *Liberation Monthly*.

Why it is blocked: Since its first publication amid the burgeoning reform protests in China, the magazine has been known for its strong support of prodemocracy activities in Hong Kong, Taiwan, and China. It famously published interviews with dissident Liu Xiaobo, including the notorious one where Liu said tongue in cheek that China might be better off under Hong Kong–style colonialism.[1] It has also published numerous books, including a set of interviews with former general secretary Zhao Ziyang while he was under house arrest and a retrospective on the 1989 Tiananmen protests. The magazine is banned in mainland China.

Note: As is the case for most Hong Kong and overseas Chinese media, the title will generally be found online written with the traditional characters 開放雜誌 (see Victoria, page 50, note 29, for more on the difference between simplified and traditional characters). While the simplified version of the name is blocked on Weibo, the traditional one is not—a curious decision, seeing as how it's usually the other way around for Hong Kong–related terms.

Other Hong Kong and overseas Chinese newspapers, which tend to be more critical of mainland China and the PRC government's policies, that have been found to be blocked include *Duowei News* (多维) and *World Journal* (世界日报).

---

1. James Fallows, "Liu Xiaobo and the '300 Years' Problem," *The Atlantic*, October 21, 2010, www.theatlantic.com/international/archive/2010/10/liu-xiaobo-and-the-300 -years-problem/64916.

遊行

(**parade**, **demonstration**, or **march** / *yóuxíng*) is a gathering of people, usually organized along a street or in a large public space. Parades are generally celebratory processions, while "demonstration" is often used to describe more political public meetings.

Why it is blocked: 遊行 is just one of many terms to describe public gatherings of people that is blocked (labor strike, 罢工 / *bàgōng*, page 138, is another), likely because it is often connected with the 1989 Tiananmen demonstrations. However, a more common variant of the word, 游行 (notice the different strokes on the left and bottom of the first character), has never been blocked. 抗议 (*kàngyì*), the general word for protest, was blocked during the summer of 2012 but unblocked otherwise, and 示威 (*shìwēi*), a common word for demonstrations, was blocked but has since been unblocked.

卫星电视

(**satellite television** / *wèixīng diànshì*) is TV programming broadcast by a communications satellite orbiting the Earth and received by households via an outdoor antenna, generally known as a satellite dish.

Why it is blocked: Installation of satellite TV dishes is regulated in China, with private ownership of them illegal in a number of cities (compelling some citizens to creatively conceal and hide theirs),[2] though workplaces that need to monitor foreign news and establishments that cater to foreigners are permitted to have them. Satellite dishes were banned in China by Li Peng in 1993, supposedly in response to Rupert Murdoch's declaration that satellite television would be "an unambiguous threat to totalitarian regimes everywhere."[3] (His company, STAR TV, which for years was stymied in its attempt to enter the Chinese market, would spend more than a decade trying to make up for that statement by apologizing for Murdoch's previous position and by cajoling Chinese officials to let them into the market.) However, those restrictions are openly flouted by residents and marketers.

Note: Satellite dishes themselves are more colloquially referred

---

2. Roland Soong, "The Digital Satellite Dishes," *EastSouthWestNorth*, August 24, 2009, zonaeuropa.com/200908b.brief.htm#007; Joe, "SARFT Outlaws Shanzhai Satellite Dishes, Chinese Reactions," *chinaSMACK*, April 26, 2010, www.chinasmack.com/2010/stories/sarft-outlaws-shanzhai-satellite-dishes-chinese-reactions.html.

3. Murdoch thought that along with the introduction of satellite television would come open access to information, and thus an inevitable shift toward a democratic society once citizens in authoritarian regimes realized what sort of options they had. "Murdoch and China," *The Observer*, August 23, 2003, www.guardian.co.uk/media/2003/aug/24/chinathemedia.rupertmurdoch.

to as woks/pots (锅 / *guō*) or plates/dishes (碟 / *dié*). The more standard word for satellite dish is 卫星天线 (天线 / *tiānxiàn* literally means "sky wire," aka antenna). 卫星天线 and 卫星碟 are not blocked on Weibo, but 卫星锅 is.

罢工

(**labor strike** / *bàgōng*) is a refusal to work by employees. It is a form of protest aimed at forcing an employer to resolve grievances or to accede to employee demands.

Why it is blocked: Though striking itself is not technically illegal under Chinese law, the right to strike was removed from the Chinese constitution in 1982 (not that strikes were tolerated before then). Therefore, unless a striker breaks other laws in conjunction with the work stoppage (which would probably be nearly unavoidable), he is technically free to strike without facing punishment.[4] Of course, since the laws do not protect strikes, work stoppages are obviously not encouraged, though there have been times where central authorities have sided with workers in efforts to pressure local officials and employers to resolve unrest.

According to official statistics, in 2009 there were 684,379 labor disputes, roughly 320,000 of which were officially dealt with in the court system.[5] Workers are also able to take their grievances to their local trade union, but the union operates as a mediator, not necessarily on the workers' behalf. Though there are no official figures for the number of strikes, it's been estimated that there are roughly 30,000–40,000 each year.[6] Strikes do take place, and in

---

4. Chang Kai, "The Legislation of Right to Strike in China," International Society for Labor and Social Security Law Eighth Asian Regional Congress, 2005, www.airroc .org.tw/ISLSSL2005/program/invited.asp.

5. Rudolf Traub-Merz, "Wage Strikes and Trade Unions in China—End of the Low-Wage Policy?," *Friedrich-Ebert-Stiftung*, June 2011, library.fes.de/pdf-files/iez/08250 .pdf.

6. "Unity Is Strength: The Workers' Movement in China, 2009–2011," *China Labour Bulletin*, October 2011, www.clb.org.hk/en/files/share/File/research_reports/unity_is _strength_web.pdf.

recent years some have been well publicized, and even successful in some cases (for example, the strikes in factories that produced Japanese auto parts and at the electronics manufacturer Foxconn in summer 2010), and there have been experiments in southern China with explicitly legalizing strikes. However, work stoppages, particularly those that attempt to involve more than one workplace, are strongly and often violently suppressed, with beatings by hired thugs, mass arrests, and prosecution of organizers.[7] Domestic media are usually barred from reporting about strikes. (For a great at-a-glance look at strikes that have been reported in recent years, see the crowdsourced map at chinastrikes.crowdmap.com.)

7. Simon Gilbert, "China's Strike Wave," *International Socialism*, June 29, 2005, www.isj.org.uk/index.php4?id=125.

组织者

(**organizer** / *zǔzhīzhě*) is a person who organizes. Like the English word, 组织者 has a mostly neutral connotation. In Chinese, it can refer to the organizer of a meeting or a conference as well as the organizer of a union or a community. It can even refer to an athlete like LeBron James or Peyton Manning who organizes teammates around him during a game.

Why it is blocked: Of course, it's not for these reasons that "organizer" is blocked; it's the organizing of labor strikes, independence movements, and political reform that worries authorities.

宪章

(**charter** / *xiànzhāng*) is a set of principles that guide the way an organization or country is run.

Why it is blocked: There is one specific charter that Chinese authorities have fought particularly hard to censor: Charter 08 (零八宪章 / *Língbā Xiànzhāng*). Published on the sixtieth anniversary of the UN Universal Declaration of Human Rights in 2008, Charter 08 presented nineteen demands to the Chinese government, including separation of powers, elimination of one-party rule, protection of the environment, free markets, guarantee of human rights, and protection of private property. The manifesto was signed by more than three hundred Chinese intellectuals and activists, many of whom were subsequently questioned, harassed, or even jailed. One of the primary authors of the document, Liu Xiaobo, was convicted of inciting subversion of state power (see page 184) and is serving eleven years in prison (see Jinzhou Prison, page 130).

推特

(**Twitter** / *Tuītè*) is an American social media . . . oh, you know what it is.

Why it is blocked: Twitter's uncontrolled stream of news, gossip, rants, and Foursquare updates terrifies Chinese officials. Twitter and other online sources of user-generated content and online sharing, such as YouTube, Facebook, Blogger, and WordPress, have the potential not just to criticize the government, but also, in a worst-case scenario for the Communist Party, to cause the overthrow of the government, as they supposedly did in Egypt in 2011. These sites are not just unsearchable on Weibo; their websites are totally unreachable[8] to the majority of Chinese Internet users.[9]

---

8. To know what websites are blocked in China, go to GreatFire.org (en.greatfire .org for the English site) or install the China Channel Firefox browser plug-in (china channel.fffff.at) to explore what it would be like to surf the web behind the Great Firewall (the older Firefox version 3 is required).

9. Those with a Virtual Private Network connection or a proxy (a mirror from a computer server in another country) enabled are able to circumvent China's Great Firewall (see page 38), but those who have such tools and bother to use them compose a very small percentage of the Chinese Internet population, which currently stands at over half a billion people. Even so, Twitter does have a tiny foothold in China, and the artist and activist Ai Weiwei maintains a very active Twitter feed that is followed by more than 170,000 people. However, a 2012 survey that estimated Twitter had more than 35 million users in China merits extreme skepticism (Tom Smith, "China: The Home to Facebook and Twitter?," *GlobalWebIndex*, September 27, 2012, globalweb index.net/thinking/china-the-home-to-facebook-and-twitter). Chinese social media scholar Isaac Mao estimates the actual number is around 100,000 (Tom Phillips, "China's Xinhua Irks Bloggers by Using Twitter," *The Telegraph*, December 12, 2012, www.telegraph.co.uk/news/worldnews/asia/china/9739038/Chinas-Xinhua-irks -bloggers-by-using-Twitter.html).

Twitter has been blocked on and off since its inception in 2006 but was permanently blocked in the run-up to June 4 in 2009. In its absence, a number of Chinese microblogs took advantage of the vacuum, including Sina Weibo, which is the most prominent, and Tencent Weibo, its major competitor. Though both started as Twitter-like clones, they have now developed into full-fledged social networking services with an array of unique features. Of course, these domestic microblog sites follow government orders to self-censor their users' posts, thus leading to the search blocks and post deletions that netizens have had to deal with.

In January 2012, Twitter publicly announced that it would comply with "valid and applicable" requests to block tweets that violated local laws.[10] Though some conjectured that this paved the way for Twitter's attempt to break into the Chinese market, with Chinese netizens already locked in to their own microblog services, the announcement was more likely aimed at markets including India and Russia, each of which has its own complex relationship with free speech and media.

---

10. "Tweets Still Must Flow," *Twitter Blog*, January 26, 2012, blog.twitter.com/2012 /01/tweets-still-must-flow.html.

毋忘

(**never forget** / *wú wàng*) is the first half of a four-character idiomatic phrase (known as a *chengyu*) from classical Chinese, 毋忘在莒 (*wú wàng zài Jǔ*), literally translated as "Don't forget that you're in Ju." Ju was a Chinese city during the Warring States Period. Under King Min, the Qi state suffered heavy losses of territory and faced defeat by the state of Yan. However, General Tian Dan regrouped his forces in the city of Ju and counterattacked, retaking Qi's lost territory. The phrase is meant to motivate a group that is on the losing side of a battle and remind it not to forget that victory is still possible.

Why it is blocked: Chiang Kai-shek's calligraphy of the phrase 毋忘在莒 was inscribed in a stone in Kinmen National Park just after he and the Nationalists fled mainland China to Taiwan in 1949 during the Chinese civil war. He hoped the words would continue to inspire the Nationalists to strive hard to recover the mainland. Today, Kinmen (also known as Jinmen in mainland China), mere miles from China's coast, is still controlled by Taiwan, but local residents hold many cultural and economic ties to the mainland.

毋忘 is also used to reference the subjugation to Western powers and Japan that China suffered during the late Qing dynasty (毋忘国耻 / "Never forget the national humiliation") as well as the June 4, 1989, crackdown in Tiananmen Square, its usage akin to how other countries use the phrase "Never forget" to memorialize a tragedy (9/11, the Holocaust, the Armenian genocide). The Tiananmen Mothers (天安门母亲), an activist group that advocates for the victims and families who lost their children on June 4, is also blocked on Weibo.

空凳

(**empty stool** / *kōngdèng*) is a reference to the empty chair between Thorbjørn Jagland and Kaci Kullmann Five during the awarding of the 2010 Nobel Peace Prize . . .

Why it is blocked: . . . an award that the recipient, Liu Xiaobo, was unable to receive because he was in prison (see charter, page 141). One of the iconic images of the evening was of the chairman of the Nobel Committee, Thorbjørn Jagland, placing the Nobel medal onto the vacant seat. Hong Kong media and netizens used the phrase as a tribute to Liu.

Coincidentally, the Hong Kong musician Danny Summer, the "father of Hong Kong rock and roll" and writer of the classic Tiananmen Square tribute song "Mama, I Didn't Do Anything Wrong," had penned an unrelated ballad to his dead father also entitled "空凳" in 1985.

快闪党

(**flash mob** / *kuài shǎn dǎng*) is a "public gathering of complete strangers, organized via the Internet or mobile phone, who perform a pointless act and then disperse again."[11] Though the concept has existed in the past, the modern version was popularized by former *Harper's* editor Bill Wasik, who organized a series of gatherings throughout New York City in 2003.[12] They were mostly social experiments or a sort of performance art, and quickly spread across the globe. This is in contrast to a "smart mob," which is more directed and typically has a goal, the *dîner en blanc* phenomenon for instance, where people dress in all white and gather at specified locations for a secret dinner.

Why it is blocked: Even though most flash mobs do nothing more harmful than show off a few Michael Jackson pelvic thrusts,[13] Chinese authorities still fear the idea of large numbers of people organizing in public spaces, perhaps viewing it as training for future political gatherings. Flash mobs, though often harmless and playful, have caused disorder and even violence in other countries, a situation authorities no doubt are keen to avert.

---

11. "Flash mob," *Oxford Dictionaries*, Oxford University Press, accessed December 17, 2012, oxforddictionaries.com/definition/english/flash%2Bmob#m_en_gb0972977.

12. Bill Wasik, "The Mob Project," BillWasik.com, May 6, 2009, billwasik.com/post/104403795/the-mob-project.

13. "Beat It" is a particularly popular choice, and flash mob versions have been performed in various locations across China. For example, see: Fauna, "Zhuhai Flash Mob Remembers Michael Jackson's Death," *chinaSMACK*, June 27, 2011, www.chinasmack.com/2011/videos/zhuhai-flash-mob-michael-jackson-memorial.html.

自由花

("**The Flower of Freedom**" / "*Zìyóu Huā*") is a Cantonese song written by Hong Kong lyricist Thomas Chow to commemorate the victims of June 4, 1989. He set the lyrics to the popular Taiwanese song "Sailor" by Zheng Zhihua.[14]

Why it is blocked: It is sung every year by those who attend the June 4 vigil at Hong Kong's Victoria Park (see page 50). From the chorus:

> But there is a dream, it will not die, remember it!
> No matter how hard the rain falls, freedom still will bloom.
> There is a dream, it will not die, remember this!

It may also be sensitive because it is a homophone for liberalization (自由化 / *zìyóuhuà*), an economic and social policy contested within the Communist Party (see New Western Hills Symposium, page 31).

---

14. You can listen to it at 8964hk, "自由花-毋忘六四 (Flower of Freedom—Never Forget June 4)," YouTube, May 29, 2006, www.youtube.com/watch?v=5GyryRRL-NY, and find sheet music for the song at "自由花 歌譜下載," Hong Kong Alliance, accessed December 17, 2012, alliance.org.hk/infoindex/song/lyrics/a01.html.

三月学运

(**March Student Movement** / *Sānyuè Xuéyùn*), otherwise known as the Wild Lily student movement, was a student-led protest that took place from March 16 to March 22, 1990, outside Memorial Square in Taipei. At the time, Taiwan, which had only just lifted a four-decade-long decree of martial law known as the "White Terror" in 1987, was still struggling to transition to a genuinely democratic government. More than three hundred thousand demonstrators occupied the square and demanded direct elections. President Lee Teng-hui met with students and offered his support. Six years later, he was re-elected in a popular vote, with more than 95 percent of eligible voters participating. Each year on March 21, democracy activists return to the square to commemorate the event.

Why it is blocked: The March Student Movement came less than a year after the Tiananmen crackdown, and the contrasts couldn't have been more stark. Like the mainland, Taiwan at the time was essentially under a one-party system and used martial law as a legal mechanism to crush dissenting opinions, which included suppressing both pro-reunification opinions and pro-independence movements.[15] However, beginning with Lee's term in office, individual

---

15. Advocating for an independent Taiwan would admit defeat and give up on the fiction that Taiwan was in fact the legitimate seat of all China, which was the position that the KMT government held in the decades following their defeat by the Communists in the Chinese civil war. Chiang Kai-shek, the leader of the KMT and president of Taiwan from 1948 until his death in 1975, feared, perhaps rightfully so, that outside elements were conspiring to support Taiwan's pro-independence movement. Therefore he relentlessly persecuted them as well as supposed Communist sympathizers, jailing more than 100,000 people and executing thousands throughout the three decades he was in power (for comparison, Taiwan had only 10 million people in 1960).

rights were gradually restored, and political reforms made Taiwan a truly democratic nation, albeit one with the typical problems of corruption and cronyism that all governments face.

Taiwanese students adopted the wild lily as their emblem because the flower symbolized fortitude and purity. It has now become an icon for democracy in Taiwan.[16] Over two decades later, another flower-named democracy movement, the so-called Jasmine Revolution, bloomed in Tunisia but was stifled in China. There was no meeting with students for Chinese officials in 2011. Instead, mentions of jasmine (茉莉花 / *mòlìhuā*) were blocked online, the sale of jasmine flowers was banned, and dozens of activists were arrested or detained by police.

---

16. Flora Wang, "Wild Lilies Slam Use of Lily Symbol," *Taipei Times*, January 7, 2008, www.taipeitimes.com/News/taiwan/archives/2008/01/07/2003396038.

五四运动

(**May Fourth Movement** / *Wǔsì Yùndòng*) was a student-led demonstration that took place in front of Tiananmen on May 4, 1919. Three thousand students from Peking University rallied against concessions that China's government made during the Paris Peace Conference negotiations after the end of World War I. The Chinese government, at the time composed of a coalition of warlords, gave up China's territory in Shandong Province to Japan even though they had been promised the land's return in exchange for fighting with the Allies. Anger spread throughout the country, and over the following months, workers and merchants joined the protests, with strikes in Shanghai crippling the economy. In the end, the Chinese ambassador, Wellington Koo, refused to sign the Versailles Treaty, and China signed a separate treaty with Germany wherein China regained Shandong.

Why it is blocked: The May Fourth Movement is hailed as a moment when China stood up to the Western powers and as the event that planted the seeds of Communism throughout the nation. It was also a celebration of new, antitraditional thinking based in science (dubbed the New Culture Movement), nationalism, and student power, which China recognized by marking May 4 as Youth Day.

However, in recent years, May 4 celebrations in some cities have been curtailed as the government has watched May 4 marches become more and more stridently anti-Japan, even violently so. In 2005, Shanghai police officers made a show of force to head off planned anti-Japan demonstrations.[17] Large demonstrations are certainly not viewed favorably by the authorities (unless they serve

---

17. Jim Yardley, "Chinese Police Head Off Anti-Japan Protests," *New York Times*, May 5, 2005, www.nytimes.com/2005/05/05/international/asia/05china.html.

the government's purpose; see Boycott Japanese goods, page 14). Angry youth can be unpredictable, and previous demonstrations that have taken place around May 4 (for instance in 1989) didn't turn out so well for the government.

Note: Though May Fourth is certainly a sensitive topic, the blocking of this particular keyword may not be intentional (see page 189 for more on the "Scunthorpe problem"): in my initial test in early 2012, any keyword containing the word 运动 (which is translated as not only "movement" or "campaign" but also as "sports" and "exercise") and 四 ("four") or 89 was blocked, an indication that it was in fact posts about June 4 campaigns that were being targeted. Thus, for some time in 2012, all sorts of innocent keywords, such as 第四届亚洲运动会 ("The Fourth Asian Games") and 1896 年夏季奥林匹克运动会 ("the 1896 Olympic Games"), were blocked along with this one about the May Fourth Movement.

学生领袖

(**student leader** / *xuéshēng lǐngxiù*) is a student who serves a leadership role in a school organization.

Why it is blocked: In the Chinese context, it refers to students who lead protest movements and demonstrations and is most commonly used to describe the organizers of the Tiananmen Square protests in 1989. Students from Peking University and Tsinghua University initiated a memorial service in Tiananmen in April 1989 after the death of the much-respected government official Hu Yaobang, who promoted political and economic reforms that the students supported, but the gathering soon evolved into a general protest. Aware of how previous student-driven protests had failed, the students decided that an organization with a unified leadership was needed. Student councils from more than fifty Beijing-area universities agreed to form the Beijing Students Autonomous Federation (also known in English as the Capital Autonomous Federation of University Students—in Chinese abbreviated as 北高联 or 高自联, both blocked on Weibo). The BSAF raised many issues, including lack of job prospects, government corruption, rising inflation, lack of individual rights, and the need for political reform. The group directed hunger strikes, which expanded the protest's recognition outside Beijing, and held meetings on how to proceed with the students' demands. Student leaders, including Wu'er Kaixi and Wang Dan, met government representatives in a televised broadcast on May 18, but the negotiations ended without any results. The documentary *The Gate of Heavenly Peace* portrayed levels of division within student ranks, especially in an interview with student leader Chai Ling. In the end, soldiers began their advance on the evening of June 3 and cleared the square on June 4. Student leaders went into hiding, and on June 13, the government issued a list of twenty-one student leaders most wanted for arrest.[18] Those who were unable to flee the country (see Operation Yellowbird, page 12) were eventually detained and served jail sentences.[19] Some continue to engage in activist work today, either in China or overseas.

18. Gerhard Joren, "The Tiananmen Students 21 Most Wanted List, Issued on June 13th, 1989," *OnAsia*, November 23, 2008, www.onasia.com/system/preview.aspx?pvp =gjo0664911.50.

19. Stacy Mosher, "Tiananmen's Most Wanted—Where Are They Now?" *CRF 2004, No.2—Tiananmen: The Once and Future China*, Human Rights in China, 2004, www.hrichina.org/crf/article/3747.

激流中国

(**Dynamic China** / *Jīliú Zhōngguó*) was a documentary television series about contemporary China that aired in Japan in 2007 and 2008. It was produced by NHK, Japan's national public broadcaster. Topics covered included the water crisis in Beijing, life at a nursing home in Qingdao, running a business in Tibet, and health care across China.

Why it is blocked: The show was praised by local critics and viewers who appreciated the series' objective take on complicated topics such as income inequality, the one-child policy, and land development. Though the Chinese government initially approved of the series for filming and broadcast, after only a few episodes it deemed the show controversial and began blocking mainland access to videos of it online. Twenty-four episodes were planned, but only thirteen were ever aired.

自由亚洲
美国之音

自由亚洲 (**Radio Free Asia** / *Zìyóu Yàzhōu*), founded in 1996, is an American nonprofit corporation that transmits radio broadcasts throughout Asia. 美国之音 (**Voice of America** / *Měiguózhīyīn*), founded in 1942, is another broadcasting organization controlled by the American government that streams localized programming around the world via radio, TV, and the Internet. Both produce cultural content and report on news stories that may be overlooked or suppressed by local authorities. Both are also supervised and funded in whole by the Broadcasting Board of Governors (BBG), an agency whose board is appointed by the president of the United States and confirmed by the Senate, and whose funding comes from congressional appropriations.

Why it is blocked: The BBG's stated mission is "to promote freedom and democracy and to enhance understanding through multimedia communication of accurate, objective, and balanced news, information and other programming about America and the world to audiences overseas."[20] China and other nations around the world have claimed that Radio Free Asia and Voice of America are nothing more than propaganda networks of the United States and that their intended aim is to topple foreign governments. In fact, in 1967 *Ramparts* magazine revealed in an exposé that a number of international broadcasting organizations including Radio Free Europe

---

20. "Fiscal Year 2010 Performance and Accountability Report," Broadcasting Board of Governors, 2010, www.bbg.gov/wp-content/media/2011/12/2010PAR.pdf.

were in fact funded by the CIA. These criticisms and allegations from the receivers' side along with claims of ineffectiveness from the American side have dogged both organizations over the years despite their accomplishments, such as the 2011 Voice of America–produced online video series *OMG! Meiyu*, which went viral among Chinese netizens. Hosted by Jessica Beinecke, the show sought to teach Chinese viewers American slang in a fun, informal way and was praised in the United States and abroad.

独立中文笔会

(Independent Chinese PEN / *Dúlì Zhōngwén Bǐhuì*) is the Chinese affiliate of PEN International, a worldwide nongovernmental organization founded in 1921 that supports writers and defends their right to free speech. There are 145 PEN Centers around the world. PEN is most well known for its awards, its literary festivals, and its Writers in Prison Committee, which advocates on behalf of persecuted and imprisoned writers around the world.

Why it is blocked: Like other PEN Centers, the Independent Chinese PEN Center (ICPC) serves both a literary function and a human rights one. It is the rights side that has brought trouble from the government: PEN documents cases of imprisoned writers, writes petition letters to authorities, provides information about imprisoned writers to other international organizations, and solicits donations for imprisoned writers.[21] Most recently, the ICPC alerted media to the detention of Jiao Guobiao (see Boxun.com, page 158), and it maintains a list of more than one hundred writers in prison,[22] one of whom is 2010 Nobel Peace Prize winner Liu Xiaobo (see empty stool, page 145), who served as president of the ICPC from 2003 until 2007.

A number of other international rights and advocacy organizations are also blocked on Weibo, including Reporters Without Borders (无国界记者 / *Wúguó jièjìzhě*) and Amnesty International (国际特赦组织 / *Guójì Tèshè Zǔzhī*).

---

21. Independent Chinese PEN Center, accessed December 17, 2012, www.chinesepen.org/english.

22. "Writers in Prison Committee—in English," Independent Chinese PEN Center, 2004, www.penchinese.com/wipc/06english/06englishl-wipl.htm, "狱中作家委员会网," Writers in Prison Committee of ICPC, accessed December 17, 2012, www.penchinese.com/wipc/index.html.

博讯

(**Boxun.com** / *Bóxùn*) is a website that accepts reader-submitted news stories and tips, posting on average ten articles a day. The website was started in 2000 by Watson Meng, a Chinese citizen who graduated from Duke University, and it is considered one of the earliest blogs in China.

Why it is blocked: Boxun publishes daily articles that mostly deal with Chinese politics. Over the past decade, the site has not shied away from controversial topics and has been blacklisted by the Great Firewall, making it unreachable for most Chinese citizens. Its writers have even been arrested, including most recently Jiao Guobiao, who was charged with "suspicion of inciting subversion of state power" (see page 184) in an article about the Diaoyu Islands dispute with Japan (see Boycott Japanese goods, page 14).[23] Its servers have also been the target of denial-of-service attacks.[24]

Since the start of the Bo Xilai scandal (see page 118), Boxun has covered the scandal so extensively and broken so many stories that there are rumors that anti-Bo insiders must be leaking information to Boxun in order to undermine Bo.[25] Thus, the site serves as a sort of WikiLeaks. Though Boxun's editors attempt to verify the

---

23. "News: China: Writer and Member of the Independent Chinese PEN Centre (ICPC) Dr Jiao Guobiao arrested," PEN International, September 19, 2012, www.pen -international.org/newsitems/china-writer-and-member-of-the-independent-chinese -pen-centre-icpc-dr-jiao-guobiao-arrested.

24. Isaac Stone Fish, "Inside Boxun, China's Media Muckraker," *Foreign Policy*, April 26, 2012, blog.foreignpolicy.com/posts/2012/04/26/inside_boxun_chinas _media_muckraker.

25. Richard McGregor and Kathrin Hille, "Chinese Censors Hamstrung by US Site," *Financial Times*, April 22, 2012, www.ft.com/intl/cms/s/0/fb55035e-8c51-11e1-9758 -00144feab49a.html#axzz2FLZe7Gce.

reader-submitted rumors and tips, some of what is published remains pure speculation. Currently, Boxun is facing a lawsuit from the actress Zhang Ziyi for publishing a story that she was a paid mistress of Bo Xilai.

The site proudly declares that it is an independent news source and is not anti-China, merely a watchdog. However, critics of the site point out that from 2005 to 2009 it received funding from the National Endowment for Democracy (NED), a U.S. organization that itself is funded entirely by the State Department. Critics of the NED allege that NED grantees are merely fronts for CIA operations designed to create turmoil in other nations.

Readers can go to en.boxun.com to browse the site's English-language content.

7

#security# #violence# #suppression#

坦克

(**tank** / *tǎnkè*) is a transliteration of the English word "tank." It is an armored vehicle first used in World War I.

Why it is blocked:

AP Images

血案

(**massacre** / *xuèàn*) is an informal term for a mass murder (the more formal, common term is 谋杀, *mousha*). It literally means "blood case."

Why it is blocked: Obviously, it is a reference to violence, though at first glance, it doesn't seem any more bloody than 谋杀, which is unblocked. However, 血案 seems to be a phrase often used to describe the 1989 Tiananmen crackdown (see East Chang'an Avenue, page 177, for more on the controversy about where protesters were killed). 屠杀 (*túshā*) is another word for massacre that is blocked for similar reasons.

东方闪电

(**Eastern Lightning** / *Dōngfāng Shǎndiàn*) aka "Real God" or "Church of Almighty God," is an offshoot Christian cult in China. The sect was founded in 1989; its followers believe that a woman born in Henan Province, known as Lightning Deng, is the second coming of Christ, and that those who do not convert will suffer awful deaths.

Why it is blocked: The Chinese government lists the group as a cult and has actively tried to suppress it, especially since its theology appears to take an explicitly antigovernment stance.[1] In addition, there are allegations that the group kidnaps, brainwashes, and bribes people to convert.[2] It is arguably the second most suppressed religion in China after the Falun Gong.

The government made renewed efforts to attack the group in 2012 after the cult reissued pronouncements that the end of the world would arrive on December 21, just as the Mayans had predicted. The group was accused of fomenting fear among the populace, and a leaked government directive exhorted news outlets to discontinue reporting on the Almighty God cult:

> [Almighty God] creates an atmosphere of social panic by spreading rumors and propagating false claims and heresies, such as

---

1. "This organization attacks China [espousing] that currently she is a large decadent emperor family dominated by the Big Red Dragon." Shixiong Li and Xiqiu (Bob) Fu, "Religion and National Security in China: Secret Documents from China's Security Sector," Committee for Investigation on Persecution of Religion in China, February 11, 2002, www.china21.org/English/docs/Final%20Report.htm.

2. Andrew Jacobs, "Chatter of Doomsday Makes Beijing Nervous," *New York Times*, December 19, 2012, www.nytimes.com/2012/12/20/world/asia/doomsday-chatter -makes-chinese-government-nervous.html.

the apocalypse. The cult seriously endangers social stability. It is essentially an anti-social, misanthropic, perverse religious sect. Recently its activities have become rather common in certain villages and towns in Xinchang, particularly in remoter areas. It has an evil influence; the need to crack down and bring it under control is acute. All levels of the government are to alert the masses to awaken to the nature of the "Real God" cult, such that they do not fall prey to the faith. When propaganda materials or individuals from this evil cult are discovered, please report this immediately to the local police station or call the police by dialing 110.[3]

---

3. Anne Henochowicz, "Ministry of Truth: The 'Almighty God Cult,'" *China Digital Times*, December 19, 2012, chinadigitaltimes.net/2012/12/ministry-of-truth-tackling-almighty-god-cult.

便衣

(**plain clothes** / *biànyī*) refers to plainclothes police: officers who wear "ordinary clothes" instead of a uniform to avoid detection or identification as law enforcement agents.

Why it is blocked: In addition to fighting crime and maintaining public security, plainclothes police (also known as undercover police) have been reported to harass and intimidate dissidents, activists, journalists, and common citizens. In August 2008, Ai Weiwei was confronted by a group of policemen and plainclothes officers while in his hotel room in Chengdu, Sichuan. The plainclothes officers beat him so badly that he suffered a brain hemorrhage. In 2011, a number of Ai's associates were also detained by plainclothes officers.[4]

---

4. Jerome A. Cohen, "The Ai Weiwei Papers," *New Statesman*, October 18, 2012, www.newstatesman.com/politics/politics/2012/10/ai-weiwei-papers.

迫害

(**persecution** / *pòhài*) is the intentional mistreatment of an individual or group, particularly those who hold differing outlooks or opinions from the majority. The mistreatment may include harassment, isolation, imprisonment, intimidation, or physical assault.

Why it is blocked: Claims of religious (e.g., Falun Gong, Christians), ethnic (Uyghur), and political (democracy activists) persecution are sensitive topics in China.

九一一袭击

(**the September 11 attacks** / *jiǔyīyī xíjī*) were a series of suicide attacks attributed to the Islamist terrorist group al-Qaeda that targeted the United States on September 11, 2001.

Why it is blocked: China has been battling its own Muslim rebels, whom it also labels terrorists, in its Western provinces. Though Chinese citizens and leaders generally expressed great sympathy and condolences to the United States following 9/11, the combination of violence, religion, and America make this a sensitive topic, regardless of China's avowed alignment with the United States in the War on Terror post-9/11.

封锁

(**blockade** / *fēngsuǒ*) is the isolation or cutting off by force of food, supplies, war matériel, or communications from a particular area.

Why it is blocked: As the Wukan "siege" showed, blockades of protesting villages and rogue towns are unflattering to China's domestic and international reputation (see violent demolition, page 179): In September 2011, several hundred citizens from Wukan village marched to the county government seat, protesting what is now a disappointingly familiar story in towns and cities all across the country: illegal land seizures by local officials, who evict residents and sell the land to developers or corporations, pocketing a fee. After a village negotiating team was kidnapped and one of the village heads died suspiciously while in police custody, thousands of citizens gathered and took to the streets. Police in riot gear were sent in to quell the protest, beating dozens, but they retreated after citizens refused to back down. Local party officials fled the village as well, and police cordoned off the newly autonomous town, laying "siege." After a tense standoff and days of exhilarating foreign press coverage, provincial-level officials stepped in and capitulated to village demands that the officials responsible for the land sell-off be dismissed.[5]

---

5. Jason Q. Ng, "So-Called 'Occupy Wukan' Wins Gains in China by Keeping Local," *Waging Nonviolence*, January 9, 2012, wagingnonviolence.org/2012/01/so -called-occupy-wukan-wins-gains-in-china-by-keeping-local.

砍刀

(**machete** / *kǎndāo*) is a large cleaverlike cutting tool, often used for agricultural purposes.

Why it is blocked: Mentally unstable knife- and cleaver-wielding men attacking schoolchildren became an unfortunate phenomenon in China in 2010, 2011, and 2012.[6] However, none of these cases specifically involved machetes (though extremists did wield machetes in a 2008 attack on a group of policemen in Kashgar, see page 172), so it may simply be a matter of Weibo's general block on many weapons.

6. "School Attacks in China (2010–2011)," Wikipedia, accessed December 18, 2012, en.wikipedia.org/wiki/School_attacks_in_the_People's_Republic_of_China.

窃听器

(**hidden microphone** / *qiètīngqì*), also commonly known as a bug, is a device that secretly transmits or records conversations.

Why it is blocked: Chinese activists and foreign officials have long been concerned about the police bureau's surveillance capabilities, especially its ability to wiretap phones. A 2011 *New York Times* article opened with an anecdote about a phone conversation being cut off after a caller said the word "protest." The story elicited much amazement at the time but has since been viewed as likely to have been a fluke occurrence, at most.[7] Even so, Chinese surveillance capabilities are quite high, and such intrusive and heavy-handed tactics are not complete fantasy. A 2012 *New York Times* story documents some of the measures U.S. officials take to prevent Chinese monitoring and hacking,[8] and Bo Xilai was accused of secretly wiretapping the conversations of top leaders, including those of Hu Jintao.[9]

---

7. Adam Minter, "Fact-Checking the *New York Times*' China Coverage [Updated]," *Shanghai Scrap*, March 23, 2011, shanghaiscrap.com/2011/03/fact-checking-the-new-york-times-china-coverage.

8. Nicole Perlroth, "Traveling Light in a Time of Digital Thievery," *New York Times*, February 10, 2012, www.nytimes.com/2012/02/11/technology/electronic-security-a-worry-in-an-age-of-digital-espionage.html.

9. David Eimer, "Bo Xilai 'Spied on China's President and Other Top Leaders,'" *The Telegraph*, April 26, 2012, www.telegraph.co.uk/news/worldnews/asia/china/9227700/Bo-Xilai-spied-on-Chinas-president-and-other-top-leaders.html.

喀什

(**Kashi** or **Kashgar** / *Kāshí*) and 库车 (**Kuqa** / *Kùchē*) are Chinese cities, both located in Xinjiang Province, home to a large percentage of China's Muslim and Uyghur population.

Why it is blocked: On August 4, 2008, sixteen Chinese police officers were killed in Kashgar. Though there are conflicting accounts, state media reported that two terrorists drove a truck into a group of officers, then attacked them with grenades and machetes. The gruesome attack, just days before the start of the Beijing Olympics, drew wide attention, with some pinning the blame on Xinjiang separatists. Six days later, violence rocked another Xinjiang city, Kuqa. Again, Xinjiang separatists were blamed, with several committing suicide by detonating bombs.

Kuqa has been blocked since at least November 2011; Kashgar's block came later, in early 2012, and was probably linked to the rioting in February 2012 that left twelve dead, just the latest in a number of destabilizing incidents in the region.

奥克托今

(**HMX**, aka octogen / *àokètuōjīn*) is a chemical high explosive, sometimes mixed with TNT (梯恩梯 / *tī'ēntī*). Common backronyms for HMX include High Melting eXplosive, Her Majesty's eXplosive, and High-velocity Military eXplosive.

Why it is blocked: According to the History Channel show *Weird Warfare*, a powder form of the explosive that could be disguised as flour (and even cooked and eaten as a pancake) was developed by the United States.[10] Chinese guerrillas successfully used it against the Japanese during World War II. As it is a weapon, it has cause to be blocked, but unlike some of the others, the Chinese word for the chemical is so obscure that a search for the first three characters (which are unblocked) and a subsequent check of the posts reveal that the four-character phrase has been used fewer than twenty times in the past two years. Of course, it's possible that censors have already deleted all such posts, but a Google or Baidu search for the term doesn't turn up much outside of chemistry references either. One wonders why the censors even bothered to block such an uncommon term.

10. afterdark anwargate, "Weird Warfare 6," YouTube, September 4, 2011, www .youtube.com/watch?v=C5yAZpzFeWw#t=289s.

血房地图

(**bloodstained housing map** / *xuèfángdìtú*) is a crowdsourced project by Chinese bloggers and activists that uses Google Maps "to plot violent housing evictions and land grabs across the country."[11]

Why it is blocked: Though the Chinese central government has at times given citizens space to publicly air their grievances regarding local land seizures (most memorably allowing state-run newspapers to report on the Chongqing "nail house" incident in 2007; see violent demolition, page 179), a project of this magnitude—one that seeks to connect local activists with each other and perhaps develop a nationwide movement—is bound to be censored. The *Wall Street Journal* wondered back in October 2010, the month the maps appeared online, how long the project might continue.[12] The map that contains only incidents verified by the creator seems to have last been edited in November 2010, but the one open to public editing is still being updated, though most of the edits are to incidents from 2010 and 2011.[13]

11. Sophie Beach, "China's Blood-Stained Property Map," *China Digital Times*, October 28, 2010, chinadigitaltimes.net/2010/10/china%E2%80%99s-blood-stained -property-map.

12. Josh Chin, "China's Blood-Stained Property Map," China Real Time Report, *Wall Street Journal* blog, October 29, 2010, blogs.wsj.com/chinarealtime/2010/10/29/chinas -blood-stained-property-map.

13. Both maps can be accessed via the *Wall Street Journal* link in note 12.

伤口

(**wound** / *shāngkǒu*) is technically an injury that punctures the skin. Informally, it can also refer to bruises or other injuries caused by blunt-force trauma. It can be accidental or intentional.

Why it is blocked: This seems like an overly broad term to be blocked, as it is a common word in Chinese that doesn't necessarily connote anything malicious. However, it could be used to describe injuries that innocent victims have suffered from overzealous security forces.

外泄

(**leak** / *wàixiè*) can be used to describe (1) leaks or spills of chemicals into the environment; (2) leaked photos, usually of a sexual nature; (3) the divulging of secret information to an outside source.

Why it is blocked: All three reasons are cause for this to be blocked in China, where transparency is not prized by the government and where one's sexual congress should remain behind closed doors.

东长安街

(**East Chang'an Avenue** / *Dōng Cháng'ān Jiē*) is the ten-lane road running just north of Tiananmen Square in Beijing. *Chang'an* means "Eternal Peace."

Why it is blocked: Early on June 4, 1989, troops marched down Chang'an Avenue in riot gear, pushing the student demonstrators out of the square. Contrary to initial notions, there is much evidence that very little actual bloodshed took place inside the square, and that most of the violence occurred in the surrounding area.[14] Jay Mathews of the *Washington Post* writes,

> A few people may have been killed by random shooting on streets near the square, but all verified eyewitness accounts say that the students who remained in the square when troops arrived were allowed to leave peacefully. Hundreds of people, most of them workers and passersby, did die that night, but in a different place and under different circumstances.[15]

However, Chang'an Avenue will forever be associated with the protests due to the iconic Tank Man (see page 162), an unidentified person who stood on the street the day after the crackdown and halted a column of tanks outside Tiananmen Square.

---

14. Malcolm Moore, "WikiLeaks: No Bloodshed Inside Tiananmen Square, Cables Claim," *The Telegraph*, June 4, 2011, www.telegraph.co.uk/news/worldnews/wikileaks/8555142/Wikileaks-no-bloodshed-inside-Tiananmen-Square-cables-claim.html.

15. Jay Mathews, "The Myth of Tiananmen," *Columbia Journalism Review*, June 4, 2010, www.cjr.org/behind_the_news/the_myth_of_tiananmen.php?page=all.

中俄密约

(**Sino-Russian Secret Treaty** / *Zhōng É Mìyuē*), also known as the Li-Lobanov Treaty, was a pact made between China and Russia in 1896. Each side promised to come to the other's aid in case it was attacked by Japan. In addition to the defensive alliance, China also made a number of other concessions to Russia, including the construction of a Russian railroad into northeastern China.

Why it is blocked: The treaty's numerous concessions to Russia and the Russian-built railroad have been blamed for helping to inflame the antiforeign sentiment that led to the Boxer Rebellion. After the signing of the Sino-Russian Secret Treaty, Russia dominated the northeastern region of China. Reminders of China's loss of sovereignty during that period are likely not appreciated today—unless of course they are used to whip netizens into a nationalistic fervor (see Boycott Japanese goods, page 14).

Anne-Marie Brady also notes that "Sino-Russian border" (中俄边界 / *Zhōng É biānjiè*) was among the items in a list of banned words uncovered in 2004.[16] In that case, the term referred to a criticized treaty that Jiang Zemin signed with Russian president Vladimir Putin in 1999 that resolved the contested boundary between the two nations. Perhaps "Sino-Russian Secret Treaty" is a critical reference to this more recent event.

---

16. Anne-Marie Brady, *Marketing Dictatorship: Propaganda and Thought Work in Contemporary China* (Lanham, MD: Rowman & Littlefield, 2008), 135.

暴力拆迁

(**violent demolition** / *bàolì chāiqiān*) is the forced eviction of residents from their property in order to knock down their homes. This typically occurs because the government wishes to develop the land.[17]

Why it is blocked: Like citizens in the United States whose properties are seized by eminent domain, Chinese residents are usually compensated for their homes and land, but often at a fraction of their future, developed worth. Furthermore, the property is sometimes used for anything but the common good. In 2011, farmers in Wukan famously expelled the corrupt local officials who had sold off cooperatively owned land to developers who built a lavish resort hotel (see blockade, page 169).

Private property rights were abolished during the Cultural Revolution, and it was only in 2004 that private property was reintroduced to Chinese law by way of an amendment to the Chinese constitution. This inviolable right to private property was further elucidated in a law adopted by the National People's Congress in 2007. However, the law continued to affirm that the state is the true owner of all land in China—citizens merely rent the use of it, seventy years at a time.

This seeming contradiction has led to numerous land disputes in China, with some residents refusing to leave, even when faced with bulldozers (online sentiment almost always sides with the property owner).[18] This has led to the phrase "nail houses" (钉子户 /

---

17. For the most comprehensive report on forced evictions in China, see Amnesty International, *Standing Their Ground: Thousands Face Violent Eviction in China* (London: Amnesty International, 2012), www.amnesty.org/en/library/asset/ASA17 /001/2012/en/976759ee-09f6-4d00-b4d8-4fa1b47231e2/asa170012012en.pdf.

18. It's been argued that this populist anger at developers and support for the "native" was part of the reason why *Avatar*, a story about a local tribe fighting back

dīngzihù) to describe what the buildings of holdouts look like as the land all around them is cleared for development—like nails left sticking out of the flattened ground. When escalating settlement payments are refused, developers and local officials may even resort to forced demolitions, rousing citizens in the middle of the night and dragging them out—if they're lucky—before demolishing their homes. If not, the property owners are crushed to death inside their homes. (See also bloodstained housing map, page 174.)

against colonizers, became the best-selling movie ever in China ("'Avatar' a Eulogy for China's 'Nail Houses,'" Xinhua, January 13, 2010, news.xinhuanet.com/english /2010-01/13/content_12804107.htm). Government officials, perhaps nervous about this sensitive interpretation of the film (but also to encourage filmgoers to see domestic movies), pulled it from theaters earlier than intended in early January 2010, but many theaters ignored the prohibition. The ban was later lifted and theaters resumed showing the film later in January (Sharon LaFraniere, "China's Zeal for 'Avatar' Crowds Out 'Confucius,'" *New York Times*, January 29, 2010, www.nytimes.com/2010/01/30 /business/global/30avatar.html).

藏人抗议

(**Tibetan protest** / *Zàngrén kàngyì*) refers to the independence movement within Tibet, a western province in China.

Why it is blocked: Like a number of other regions in China with large minority populations (see West Ujimqin, page 22, note 23), Tibet is administered with particular care by the Chinese government. The complex relationship between the two stretches back centuries and has alternated between periods of peace and extreme conflict, especially since the formation of modern China.[19] In March 2008, a series of ethnic riots rocked the Tibetan capital of Lhasa and led to much protest by Tibetans and foreigners alike in the run-up to the 2008 Beijing Olympics that summer (see Boycott Carrefour, page 14).

---

19. This is putting it much too simply. For more on China's relationship with Tibet, try Melvyn C. Goldstein's *The Snow Lion and the Dragon: China, Tibet, and the Dalai Lama* (Berkeley: University of California Press, 1997).

钴-60

(**cobalt-60** / *gŭ-60*) is a radioactive isotope of the metal cobalt. It is used for sterilizing medical equipment, medical radiation in treating cancer patients, and irradiating food, among other uses.

Why it is blocked: Though cobalt-60 has a number of legitimate uses, it can also be highly toxic when not carefully controlled. Unmanaged exposure to cobalt-60 can lead to burns, radiation sickness, and even death. It is theorized that cobalt-60 could be utilized to produce a "dirty bomb." The most notable case of cobalt-60 radiation in recent years took place in 2000, when a piece of stolen medical equipment containing cobalt-60 was sold to a Bangkok scrapyard. The cobalt-60 was accidentally exposed and three junkyard workers died.

In early 2009, China announced it would begin domestic production of cobalt-60 in Zhejiang Province, increasing worldwide production by 10 percent.[20] In an unfortunate coincidence, in October of that year, a sterilization lab in Guangzhou had a malfunction and the radioactive cobalt-60 material was exposed for forty-eight days.[21] Government officials ordered local reporters to issue only terse one-sentence-long updates, and outraged residents didn't discover that they'd been exposed until December.

---

20. Terry Gangcuangco, "Cobalt-60 Will Now Be Produced by China," *Asian Power*, January 22, 2009, asian-power.com/power-utility/news/cobalt-60-will-now-be-produced-china.

21. Joel Martinsen, "Cobalt-60 Front Page Story Removed from Southern Metropolis Daily," *Danwei*, December 15, 2009, www.danwei.org/media_regulation/cobalt-60_front_page_story_rem.php.

空警200

(**KJ 200** / *Kōng Jǐng 200*) literally means "Sky Police 200." It is a Chinese military aircraft that serves as an airborne radar system for tracking enemy and friendly movement as well as for performing surveillance.

Why it is blocked: Apparently discussing this particular advanced military vehicle is sensitive. It may also be because of a high-profile crash of one of these planes in 2006. Forty military personnel and technicians died and nearly a dozen high-ranking officers were punished for the accident.[22]

---

22. Joseph Kahn, "China's Bid to Expand Air Defense Takes Hit," *New York Times*, June 6, 2006, www.nytimes.com/2006/06/06/world/asia/06iht-crash.1899967.html.

煽动颠覆
国家政权罪

(**inciting subversion of state power** / *shāndòng diānfù guójiā zhèngquán zuì*) is a specific crime in the Chinese legal code, akin to sedition (see also criminalization of speech, page 54). The law states:

> Anyone who uses rumor, slander or other means to encourage subversion of the political power of the State or to overthrow the socialist system, shall be sentenced to fixed-term imprisonment of not more than five years. However, the ringleaders and anyone whose crime is monstrous shall be sentenced to fixed-term imprisonment of not less than five years.[23]

Why it is blocked: Its vague language has been criticized by the UN,[24] and the law has been used by authorities to jail dissidents, most famously Nobel Peace Prize winner Liu Xiaobo (empty stool, page 145) in 2009.

Of note is that this is one of the longest unique phrases blocked on Weibo.

23. Wei Luo, trans., *The 1997 Criminal Code of the People's Republic of China* (Buffalo, NY: William S. Hein, 1998), 73.

24. UN Commission on Human Rights, *Addendum to the Report Submitted by the Working Group on Arbitrary Detention: Visit to the People's Republic of China*, December 22, 1997, E/CN.4/1998/44/Add.2, www.unhcr.org/refworld/country,,,MISSION,CHN,,45377b804,0.html.

8

#misc# #why?#

毛腊肉

(**hair bacon** / *máo làròu*) is a reference to Mao Zedong's body, which is on display at the Mausoleum of Mao Zedong in Tiananmen Square, Beijing. The character 毛 means hair, but is also Mao's surname. 腊肉 translates in English to "bacon," but literally means "preserved meat." Thus, **the preserved meat of Mao**: his embalmed body, which is publicly displayed in a mausoleum on Tianamen Square. The term is generally used in a derogatory fashion.

Why it is blocked: Referring to Mao as a slab of meat is undoubtedly offensive to a government that still officially reveres the Great Helmsman, though only 70 percent of the time according to Deng Xiaoping.[1]

More: Among the top results for 毛腊肉 is a facetious recipe for how to prepare preserved Mao meat.[2] The instructions (a rough translation):

> Ingredients: a fierce boar from Huguang.[3] Steps: first, empty the internal organs and wash with 7 kg of salt, 0.2 kg of saltpeter [a nitrate food preservative], 0.4 kg pepper. For the deboned meat, use 2.5 kg salt, 0.2 kg fine saltpeter, 5 kg of sugar, 3.7 kg of *baijiu*[4] and soy sauce mixed with 3–4 kg of water. Optional ingre-

1. Richard McGregor, *The Party: The Secret World of China's Communist Rulers* (New York: HarperPerennial, 2012), 245.

2. 好好先生, "毛腊肉是什么呢？" 问问, 搜搜 (*Soso*), October 21, 2010, wenwen.soso .com/z/q228298065.htm.

3. Huguang is the traditional name for Hubei and Hunan Provinces, where Mao was born.

4. A sorghum-based liquor that Mao was well known for enjoying. The Moutai (or Maotai) brand of *baijiu* in particular has become a staple at state functions, partly due to its Revolutionary-era image. Mark McDonald, "One Chinese Liquor Brand Is

dients that can be added prior include salt and crushed pepper, fennel, cinnamon and other spices; dry and flatten, seal up well, and bathe in Chinese medicine for three days, until the surface fluffs up; that way the seasoning penetrates through the meat. Then disinfect it with grain alcohol and dry in the sun.[5]

the Life of the Party," *International Herald Tribune/New York Times*, July 3, 2012, rendezvous.blogs.nytimes.com/2012/07/03/one-chinese-liquor-brand-is-the-life-of -the-party.

5. Following this part are various descriptions of how to eat it and what it tastes like; a more recent post of this recipe adds this line: "Because of the special preservation, you can store it for up to a year; I've heard that families can even preserve Mao bacon in a jar for 40 years," the jar being, no doubt, a reference to Mao's glass enclosure. 征东讨逆大将军, "[转帖] 菜谱, 毛腊肉," 汉民族门户网 (*Han Net*), March 5, 2012, http://www.bbs.hanminzu.org/forum.php?mod=viewthread&tid=296309.

三色猫

(**tortoiseshell cat** or **calico cat** / *sānsèmāo*) literally means "tricolor cat."

Why it is blocked: Actually, a search for any colored cat, so long as it uses the term "色貓," is blocked. This is a reference to Deng Xiaoping's famed 1961 proverb in favor of market reforms: "It doesn't matter if the cat is black or white; so long as it catches mice it's good" (不管黑猫白猫能捉到老鼠的就是好猫, or something similar: searching for the term shows several variations)—the mouse being economic prosperity and national advancement, and the cat being the economic system used to achieve it. Perhaps the term was previously used to mock the current system of "socialism with Chinese characteristics." Regardless, it is now apparently a sensitive topic (though you can freely perform a search for Deng's proverb itself).

加拿大法语

(**Canadian French** / *Jiānádà Fǎyǔ*) is a term referring to the varieties of French spoken in Canada.

Why it is blocked: It's caught because of a word it unintentionally contains: 大法 (*dàfǎ*), whose standard meaning is "national constitution" but that is also an abbreviation for Falun Dafa (法轮大法), aka Falun Gong (法轮功), the outlawed cult. Similarly, a nickname for China's most prestigious law school, 人大法学院 (Renmin University of China Law School / *Réndà Fǎxuéyuàn*), is also blocked. This is an example of the Scunthorpe problem, where certain types of simple filtering algorithms block innocent terms that happen to contain banned words from a blacklist, so named for the English town of Scunthorpe, whose residents were prevented from signing up to AOL in 1996 because the word "cunt" was on AOL's blacklist. Thus, the blocking of Canadian French and Renmin Law School are mistakes but unavoidable based on the current way Weibo implements its search blocks.

伊斯兰

(**Islam** / *Yīsīlán*) is the monotheistic religion articulated by the Qur'an. Adherents live in every region in China. The highest concentrations are found in the northwest provinces of Xinjiang, Gansu, and Ningxia.

Why it is blocked: Though the state government is by all appearances atheist,[6] the Chinese constitution supports "freedom of religious belief" and officially sanctions five religions: Buddhism, Taoism, Islam, Catholicism, and Protestantism. Of these, Islam is the only one that is blocked on Weibo, likely due to tension in regions such as Xinjiang (see Kashi, page 172), where Uyghur Muslims represent roughly half the population and have pressed for greater autonomy from the central government and protested against discrimination, even going as far as rioting.

---

6. Preeti Bhattacharji, "Religion in China," Council on Foreign Relations, May 16, 2008, www.cfr.org/china/religion-china/p16272#p3.

Hoobastank

Hoobastank is an American rock band popular during the first decade of the twenty-first century. An informal poll conducted by the Seattle newspaper *The Stranger* found the band's name to be one of the worst of all time.[7]

Why it is blocked: Unfortunately, as amusing as the thought might be, it's not because Weibo censors have declared the band's style of modern rock music to be unlistenably bad; rather, the blocked keyword is "stank," and Hooba*stank* is merely caught inadvertently (see Scunthorpe problem in Canadian French, page 189). One might rightfully think the trigger would be the word "tank," the Chinese version of the word (坦克) having been blocked (see page 162), but "tank" was tested at the same time as "Hoobastank" and "tank" was unblocked. Thus, "stank" is definitely the blocked word, perhaps because of its connotations of licentiousness, since neither "stink" nor "stunk" is blocked. Or, perhaps even more likely, someone screwed up.

---

7. Grant Brissey, "Band Names: The Worst of the Worst," *The Stranger*, December 14, 2009, www.thestranger.com/lineout/archives/2009/12/14/band-names-the-worst-of -the-worst.

幸運☆星

(*Lucky Star* / *xìngyùn xīng*) is a Japanese manga (aka comic book) by Kagami Yoshimizu. It features the stories of four Japanese high school girls. An anime series, novel, and video game have since been produced based on the manga.

Why it is blocked: No idea. Both the series and the manga are for all ages and feature nothing scandalous. *Lucky Star* has become a huge hit in Japan. Hong Kong's ATV airs the series, but it doesn't appear to have crossed into mainland China. Perhaps the potential for naughty schoolgirl mashups causes this to be banned?

Because of typographical issues, the series is sometimes referred to as 幸運星, without the star. However, the proper translated title includes the star (Japanese title: らき☆すた, or transliterated into English as *Raki☆Suta*). Regardless of how one writes it, it appears that the series is targeted and is not some unintentional block.

军阀

(**warlord** / *jūnfá*) is a person who has both military and civilian authority over an area within a nation. A warlord draws power from armed forces who are loyal to him and not to the central authority. Chinese history is replete with cases of warlords fomenting rebellion (or valiantly defending their territory, depending on the victor's point of view), in particular during the Three Kingdoms Era and the period from the end of the Qing Dynasty to reunification in 1928, known as the Warlord Era.

Why it is blocked: This is another case of a noncontemporary word seemingly being unnecessarily blocked. China did reach one of its weakest points during the terrible infighting of the Warlord Era, and Chiang Kai-shek's defeat of the warlords is often credited to the Kuomintang (KMT) and not to the Chinese Communist Party, which contributed troops and resources while allied with the KMT as the First United Front. But the block is probably due to netizens comparing their corrupt and abusive local leaders to warlords.

膏药旗

(**medicine patch flag** / *gāoyàoqí*) is slang used to refer to the Japanese flag in a derogatory fashion.

Why it is blocked: 膏药 is a Chinese medicinal patch, like a large Band-Aid that comes prepackaged with an ointment used to treat aches and pains. Because the backside of many patches resembles the famous sun disc image of the Japanese flag, it is used pejoratively to refer to the Japanese flag, akin to calling the German flag *Schwarz-Rot-Mostrich* ("black-red-mustard"). Though technically on friendly terms today, Japan and China share a fraught past (see Boycott Japanese goods, page 14), with the Japanese invasions during the First Sino-Japanese War and World War II still not forgiven by most Chinese, leading to flashpoints like former Japanese prime minister Junichiro Koizumi's annual visits to the Yasukuni Shrine[8] and controversy in 2005 over Japan's adoption of textbooks that reportedly glossed over the country's World War II atrocities. More recently, in September 2010, a Chinese fishing trawler collided with a Japanese coast guard boat in disputed waters. An international incident was touched off when Japan initially detained the trawler's crew but later released them after facing intense Chinese diplomatic pressure and mass protest by Chinese citizens. A similar sequence of events took place in August–September 2012. After the Japanese government was pressured into purchasing the disputed Diaoyu Islands from the

---

8. The shrine is dedicated to Japan's war heroes and martyrs. Fourteen of the people enshrined there are convicted war criminals from World War II. China and Korea have both protested the visits to the shrine by Japanese politicians, claiming that such visits are provocative and more evidence of Japanese attempts to whitewash the country's past atrocities.

private citizens who owned them,[9] Chinese citizens retaliated by rioting across the country, targeting and vandalizing Japanese businesses and cars.

In an indication of how complex China-Japan relations are, the Chinese government had to tamp down its own protesters in 2005 and 2010 in order to control anti-Japanese fervor—this after being accused of encouraging that very behavior earlier. However, to block 膏药旗, a seemingly minor slight relative to the other obscenities hurled toward Japan online, is curious considering no other similar anti-Japan words have been found to be blocked. (One of the most common anti-Japanese insults, 日本鬼子, roughly translated as "Japanese devils," has more than seven hundred thousand search results on Weibo, and another insult, 小日本, has over 14 million.)

---

9. For all the fiscal cliff drama and political gridlock in Washington, at least the United States didn't have to deal with a rogue governor dictating foreign policy and instigating hostilities with a neighboring superpower the way Japan did in 2012. Tokyo's controversial governor Shintaro Ishihara unilaterally decided to buy the Diaoyu Islands from the Japanese citizens who privately owned them in order to claim the territory officially for Japan. Such a maneuver upended the status quo, and China had long threatened retaliation if Japan ever took such steps. However, with the purchase of the islands a fait accompli, the Japanese government was forced to intervene and buy the islands—lest it look like a regional governor was running the show, which, in fact, Ishihara was doing. The situation would be akin to Texas governor Rick Perry deciding to annex some desolate border town in Mexico (solely to infuriate Washington and to gain local popularity), leaving President Barack Obama with only one option if he didn't want to appear weak and not in control: to claim it first on behalf of America, after which Mexicans rioted and the Mexican government warned that the act was a provocation for war. "Central Government Plans to Buy Senkaku Islands," *Asahi Shimbun*, July 7, 2012, ajw.asahi.com/article/behind_news/politics/AJ 201207070062.

天葬

(**sky burial** / *tiānzàng*) is a Tibetan funeral practice where the corpse is placed on a mountainside and ritually cut with cleavers. The dead body is then left exposed, oftentimes to be eaten by waiting vultures. Sky burial is a practice that is both practical (the ground in Tibet is usually too hard to dig and fuel for cremation is scarce) and spiritual.

Why it is blocked: Disposal of the dead has at times been a contentious issue in China. Though traditionally Chinese have preferred to bury their dead in the ground, Mao initiated a campaign in the 1950s to encourage citizens to cremate corpses in order to free up more productive farmland (a notion that is still advocated today[10]) as well as to stamp out "superstitious" folk religions. In some areas, burials are still technically illegal, though such laws are widely ignored. Cremation rates have risen since the 1950s (now at 48 percent[11]), and today most urban Chinese cremate, while many of those in the countryside prefer burial.

Sky burials, also known as celestial burials or open-air burials, have the added sensitive element of being a Tibetan practice. To those who are unfamiliar with the ritual, it may also appear to be a particularly grotesque one. In 2006, in order to protect and respect the act, the central government reportedly implemented regulations, with a ban on photography and media coverage of any such burials. However, numerous photos persist online. The term is likely blocked due to the graphic and potentially upsetting nature of these images to non-Tibetans.

---

10. Xinhua, "Cremation Called for Saving Land Resources," China.org.cn, December 19, 2006, www.china.org.cn/english/government/193044.htm.

11. "International Cremation Statistics 2008," Cremation Society of Great Britain, March 28, 2011, www.srgw.demon.co.uk/CremSoc5/Stats/Interntl/2008/StatsIF.html.

敏感

(**sensitive** / *mǐngǎn*) is an adjective that means susceptible to or quick to notice slight changes, describes a person that is easily offended, or describes an issue that might cause offense.

Why it is blocked: This falls under the "don't talk about the censorship regime" category. Discussing how sensitive a topic is would inevitably remind others that sensitive topics are being censored.

共狗

(**Communist dog** / *gònggǒu*) is a derogatory insult for a Communist Party member in China. Like 共匪 (Communist bandit / *gòngfěi*), 赤匪 (red bandit / *chìfěi*), and 毛匪 (Mao's bandit / *máofěi*), it carries roughly the same connotation as "dirty Commie" in English or "damned Yankee" in the Confederacy during the American Civil War.

Why it is blocked: The three "bandit" words above were commonly used by the Nationalist Kuomintang Party during the Chinese civil war to attack Mao and his Communist supporters; thus, besides being insulting to the only significant political party in China,[12] the words carry an extra historical and political burden. These three terms are also blocked.

---

12. China technically has a number of officially registered minority parties that are able to participate in the National People's Congress, including the remains of the KMT Party, but because of the political structure and Communist Party dominance, they are little more than rubber-stampers and exist only for appearance's sake.

干你妈

(literally, **dry your mother** / *gān nǐ mā*), 操你 (literally, **grasp you** / *gān nǐ*), and 草你妈 (literally, **grass your mother** / *cào nǐ mā*) are all ways of expressing the equivalent of the English language's most potent and flexible profanity: **fuck**.

Why it is blocked: These are just a few of the colorful profanities and obscenities available to Chinese speakers.[13] A handful of these are blocked on Weibo, especially those dealing with sex acts and genitalia.

草你妈 is an especially noteworthy one because of an Internet meme involving a play on the words in 2009. As Chinese netizens are wont to do when faced with censors blocking offensive words and pruning improper posts, they form homophones out of sensitive words, transforming them into nonoffensive ones that, when read in context, make obvious what the writer is trying to convey. Thus, 草你妈 became 草泥马 (*cǎo ní mǎ*), literally, a grass mud horse. An extensive backstory and a history were created for this invented creature, which according to an article in Baidu Baike (the Chinese equivalent of Wikipedia) is a type of alpaca.[14] Such creatures supposedly resided in the Gobi Desert and were in a battle with "river crabs" (see page 203). A series of popular videos featuring alpacas and double entendre–filled song lyrics made the rounds in China in March 2009 before they were blocked.[15] Later

13. "Mandarin Chinese Profanity," Wikipedia, accessed December 13, 2012, en.wiki pedia.org/wiki/Mandarin_Chinese_profanity.

14. "草泥马," 互动百科, December 10, 2012, www.baike.com/wiki/%E8%8D%89%E6 %B3%A5%E9%A9%AC.

15. skippybentley, "Song of the Grass-Mud Horse (Cao Ni Ma)," YouTube, March 12, 2009, www.youtube.com/watch?v=wKx1aenJK08.

in the month, all of YouTube was blocked in China, which may have been due in part to the popularity of these videos.[16] Searching for 草泥马 on Youku, the leading video-sharing website in China, returns an error message, not surprisingly, warning that search results cannot be shown due to "related laws and regulations."

16. "Government Blocks Access to YouTube," Reporters Without Borders, March 25, 2009, en.rsf.org/china-government-blocks-access-to-25-03-2009,30667.html.

支那

(**Zhina** / *Zhīnà*) is the transcribed Chinese form of an ancient Sanskrit Buddhist name for China (चीन). It's thought that the Sanskrit word originated from the name of China's first dynasty, the Qin, or perhaps the famed ancient state of Jing, which in turn became the basis for China's name in other languages (چین or Čīn in Middle Persian and Sina in Latin, the root of English words such as "sinology" and "sinicize"). 支那 as a term for China was adopted by Chinese and Japanese alike, and at one point it was proposed that the Romanized name for China actually be "Shina," which is a transliteration of 支那 from Japanese.

Why it is blocked: Usage of 支那 has fallen out of favor in both China and Japan because it has taken on a derogatory tone toward Chinese people. Though not necessarily an explicit insult, the very fact that a speaker chooses to use such an outdated word when there are a number of more common alternatives available (in Japanese kanji as 中華民國, pronounced Chūka Minkoku, or in katakana, ちゅうか, pronounced Chūgoku) usually means that the speaker is making a veiled but easily decoded statement. It's somewhat akin to an American speaker using the word "Negro" or "Chinaman" today.

How it went from being a name for China commonly used by revolutionary Chinese patriots like Sun Yat-sen, the celebrated founder of modern China, to being capable of arousing a media firestorm in 2010 when newspapers reported on a Beijing shop with a poster bearing the characters is unsurprising: perceived cultural imperialism. Throughout the early twentieth century, as 支那 developed derogatory undertones during both Sino-Japanese wars, Chinese writers and officials insisted that their Japanese counterparts drop usage of 支那 and use their preferred nomenclature. Japan did not and the once harmless 支那 morphed into an actual slur (alongside continued usage as a common word). Thus, from the Chinese perspective, all usages of 支那 became colored, though Japanese speakers may not be aware of this, thinking the word is simply an old-fashioned one. For more on the history of the word, read Joshua A. Fogel's lively "New Thoughts on an Old Controversy: Shina as a Toponym for China."[17]

---

17. It wasn't until the Allied occupation of Japan that Japan accepted China's official demand to drop usage of the term Shina (Joshua A. Fogel, "New Thoughts on an Old Controversy: Shina as a Toponym for China," *Sino-Platonic Papers* 229, August 2012, www.sino-platonic.org/complete/spp229_shina_china.pdf).

溪蟹

(**river crab** / *héxiè*) commonly refers to the Chinese mitten crab, an edible crustacean native to China's eastern coast. It has now spread to waters in America and Europe, where it is considered an invasive pest. The crab is a delicacy in Chinese cuisine.

Why it is blocked: Besides its fondness for overtaking other species' habitats, the river crab is guilty of one other major sin: having a similar pronunciation to the Chinese word for harmony, 和谐. Harmony, or the "harmonious society," was the principle message of Hu Jintao's time in office. In October 2006, after the Central Committee's annual plenary session, the committee called for a re-prioritization of social stability over economic growth, with more emphasis on solving the rural-urban divide, protecting the environment, and addressing possible political reform.

Netizens were more skeptical and mocked the so-called call for a harmonious society. However, because Internet censors caught on and quickly deleted or blocked critical posts containing 和谐, netizens resorted to using "river crab" at first as a sort of code and later as a form of slang and protest. News reports have been "river crabbed" (that is, "harmonized," a euphemism for censored), and posts discuss how the invasive river crab is wrecking the country. This sort of punning is done on a whole array of words to evade the censors.

洪家楼

(**Sacred Heart Cathedral** / *Hóngjiālóu*) is in Jinan, the capital of Shandong Province. It is the largest church in the region and home of the Roman Catholic Archdiocese of Jinan. It is a major landmark of Jinan.

Why it is blocked: The church was built between 1901 and 1905 and financed by reparations China had to pay foreign nations after being defeated in the Boxer Rebellion. A number of nations offered essentially to forgive China's indemnity in acts of goodwill; for example, the United States remitted its share to support the building of Tsinghua University, and Great Britain used its share to assist in railway construction in China. Perhaps the cathedral carries with it a reminder of that humiliating period for China?

The cathedral was closed from 1966 to 1985 due to the anti-Western and antireligion fervor of the Cultural Revolution. Catholicism is no longer a persecuted religion in China (though all religions continue to be regulated and supervised by the state), and it is estimated that there are more than 12 million Catholics in China.[18] Other major Catholic cathedrals in China, including those in Guangzhou, Shanghai, and Qingdao, are not blocked on Weibo.

---

18. In China, Catholicism is seen as a distinct religion separate from Protestantism.

防洪纪念塔

(**flood control monument** / *fánghóng jìniàntǎ*) is short for 哈爾濱市人民防洪勝利紀念塔—the People's Flood Control Victory Monument in Harbin. Harbin is a major city in northeast China famous for its Russian legacy and influence, which is evident in the city's architecture, cuisine, and culture.

The monument, which anchors Stalin Park, was built in 1958 to commemorate and celebrate the city's successful battle against a flood—unlike a previous flood in 1932, which drowned tens of thousands. The monument is composed of a Roman column with a statue of heroes atop it, surrounded by twenty more columns that form a semicircle in the square. The base is made of rock, symbolizing the citizens' solid defense of the city from the raging waters, and lines at the base indicate the high-water marks in 1932, 1958, and 1998—when record-breaking waters reached nearly fifteen feet above sea level.

Why it is blocked: The exact reason is obscure to me. The monument is a major landmark in Harbin and the square is a popular outdoor space for performances, exercise, and relaxation. No doubt it is also a popular place for potential collective actions, and perhaps it was a call for some protest at the monument that caused it to be blocked.

彭博社

(**Bloomberg** / *Péngbóshè*) is a privately held American financial software, media, and data company. Bloomberg L.P. was founded by Michael Bloomberg (three-term mayor of New York City).

Why it is blocked: A number of foreign media outlets are blocked on Weibo, including Voice of America, the *World Journal*, and the *Epoch Times*, but Bloomberg is notable in that it might be considered an apolitical media corporation. Chinese authorities blocked Bloomberg's website in June 2012 after it published an exposé on the wealth accumulated by future president Xi Jinping's family,[19] but this search block on Weibo predates that article. Currently, one is unable to make a post that contains 彭博社. Trying to do so will return the error message "Sorry, this content violates 'Sina Weibo's Community Guidelines' or related regulations and policies."

19. Paul Mozur, "Bloomberg Is Inaccessible on China Web," *Wall Street Journal*, June 29, 2012, online.wsj.com/article/SB100014240527023048307045774965406296 28810.html.

驗 證 碼

(**CAPTCHA** / *yànzhèngmǎ*) is a computer-based challenge-response test used to ensure that the respondent is a human and not a robot in another computer. It usually comes in the form of a series of distorted characters that a computer user must successfully decipher and retype. CAPTCHA stands for "Completely Automated Public Turing test to tell Computers and Humans Apart." In Chinese, it literally means "verification code."

Why it is blocked: No idea. The whole phrase is blocked, not just the portion meaning "verify," and I don't know of any hidden meanings for the word. The simplified version of the characters (验证码) is not blocked. Any guesses would be appreciated.

(**conquered nation** / *wángguó*) can be translated as "vanished country" or a state heading for destruction/downfall. It's generally used to describe when an outside power has defeated a nation in war, either wiping it out or causing it to lose its independence. Examples include the overthrow of the Hawaiian Kingdom by the United States, the conquering of the First Persian Empire by Alexander the Great, and the subjugation of the Korean Empire by Imperial Japan in 1910. It is also the Chinese title of the somewhat controversial 2005 Japanese action thriller *Aegis* (*Bôkoku no îjisu*).

Why it is blocked: Perhaps the term is used by Tibetans or citizens in Xinjiang to describe Chinese control of their province? Or maybe netizens use it to insult the future state of China or to describe instances of China appearing to bow to outside/American influence? The term popped up in several news reports related to China's April 2012 dispute with the Philippines in the South China Sea. However, it is also widely used in an apolitical manner, often to describe something that is extinct or a situation wherein someone is suppressing another.

维勒

(Friedrich **Wöhler** or **Villar**-Perosa submachine gun) are examples of phonetic transliterations of Western words and names that contain the characters 维勒 (*wéilēi*). For instance, the characters make up the last name of German chemist Friedrich Wöhler (弗里德里希·维勒) and part of Colombian golfer Camilo Villegas's last name (维勒加斯).

Why it is blocked: However, it's unlikely that the characters are blocked because of either person's contributions to science or sport (though Villegas was involved in a rather racy—by Chinese standards at least—partially nude photo shoot for *ESPN the Magazine*'s 2010 "Body Issue"). More plausibly, it may be because 维勒 represents 维勒·帕洛沙—the Villar-Perosa submachine gun. Though this would be in keeping with Weibo's censorship of weapons, the Villar-Perosa is almost always referred to by its full name even in Chinese, making it strange to block just 维勒 if the intention was to control references to the weapon (which are very few). The gun was never widely used in China or anywhere except during World War I—though innovative, apparently it was a terribly ineffective gun. So the reason 维勒 is blocked is obscure.

增补

(**augment** or **supplement** / *zēngbǔ*) is a verb used to describe the addition of something new to an already existing composition.

Why it is blocked: This one is also baffling. The top results for 增补 on Google relate to the Hong Kong Supplementary Character Set (HKSCS), a local extension of the Big 5 character set encoding developed by a collaborative group of Taiwanese companies. Adopting certain character-set standards can be controversial; for instance, Japanese and Chinese techies, linguists, and culture warriors have battled over "Han unification" in the Unicode encoding set for some time.[20] However, though HKSCS does touch on potentially sensitive issues like "one country, two systems" (see Victoria, page 50, and Article 23, page 24), there doesn't appear to be any actual backlash to it.

---

20. Because Japanese, Korean, and Vietnamese writing all draw from Chinese characters but have evolved separately, certain characters have morphed in varying ways. When compared side by side, these characters are still obviously the same, but have subtle differences, somewhat akin to how serif fonts of the same letter are different from sans-serif fonts. For more specifics about this, see: "Han Unification," Wikipedia, accessed October 25, 2012, en.wikipedia.org/wiki/Han_unification; Ken Whistler, "On the Encoding of Latin, Greek, Cyrillic, and Han," *Unicode Technical Notes*, October 25, 2010, www.unicode.org/notes/tn26.

黑天使

(**black angel** or **dark angel** / *hēi tiānshǐ*) is the title of numerous novels, films, songs, and other media. *Dark Angel* is perhaps best known as the title of the Jessica Alba TV show about a genetically enhanced soldier who is on the run from the government.

Why it is blocked: Perhaps due to its association with Satan? Or with the 2002 Italian erotic art film *Senso '45*, titled *Black Angel* for overseas release? Or perhaps it's slang for prostitute or some other sensitive topic that I'm not familiar with. In the end, it may just be that someone fell asleep at the wheel and added this by accident.

色豹

(color of leopard / *sèbào*) describes things that have a leopard-spotted patterning, perhaps better translated into English as "animal print" or "leopard print."

Why it is blocked: No idea. A few animals and plants contain the phrase 色豹 in them, including the bicolor toadfish and the starfish flower (each exhibits animal-print patterns). However, it doesn't seem to be associated with anything more scandalous than, say, a pair of leopard-print bikini briefs.

Chinese Words Used, English Translation, and Weibo Block Status

All the words noted as blocked in this book were discovered to have been blocked at some point during 2011–12. For the latest status on whether the word is still blocked or not, you can go to s.weibo.com and try searching for it yourself, or go to en.greatfire.org to see a history of when certain words were blocked and unblocked. For reference, below is a list of the sensitive Chinese words mentioned in this book along with whether or not they were blocked as of October 2012.

1. #government# #CCP# #politics# #nationalism#

CHINESE	ENGLISH	BLOCKED AS OF OCTOBER 2012?
江泽民	Jiang Zemin	Yes
元老	Eight Elders	No
中联办	Liaison Office	Yes
政变	coup d'état	Yes
上海帮	Shanghai Gang	Yes
团派	the Youth League faction	Yes
黄雀行动	Operation Yellowbird	Yes
抵制日货	Boycott Japanese goods	No
抵制家乐福	Boycott Carrefour	Yes

太上皇	Retired Emperor / backstage ruler	Yes
太子党	princelings	Yes
令计划	Ling Jihua	Yes
新左派	the New Left	Yes
西乌旗	West Ujimqin	Yes
二十三条	Article 23	Yes
二月逆流	February Countercurrent	Yes
宪政民主	constitutional democracy	Yes
民族问题	minority problem	Yes
红色恐怖	red terror	Yes
雪山狮子	snow lion flag	Yes
新西山会议	New Western Hills Symposium	No
中国泛蓝联盟	the Union of Chinese Nationalists	Yes

2. #dissent# #censorship# #justice#

CHINESE	ENGLISH	BLOCKED AS OF OCTOBER 2012?
五毛	50 Cent Party	Yes
四君子	the Four Gentlemen	Yes
翻墙	over the Great Firewall	Yes
无界网络	Ultrasurf	Yes
⠌	Combining Cyrillic Millions	Yes
屄	cunt	Yes
胡	Hu (Jintao)	Yes
习	Xi (Jinping)	Yes
维基揭密	WikiLeaks	Yes
维基揭密	WikiLeaks	Yes
国新办	State Council Information Office	Yes
真理部	Ministry of Truth	Yes

CHINESE	ENGLISH	
民主墙	Democracy Wall	Yes
民主女神	Goddess of Democracy	Yes
盘古乐队	Pangu	Yes
維多利亞	Victoria	Yes
五月三十五	May 35	Yes
四號	day four	No
六月初	the beginning of June	No
liusi	six four	Yes
第四	the fourth	No
35号	day 35	Yes
四突擊	four assault	No
四运动	four movement	Yes
四事件	four event	Yes
四號戰车	day four tanks	No
绿坝娘	Green Dam Girl	No
因言获罪	criminalization of speech	Yes
宪法法院	constitutional court	Yes
四二六社论	April 26 editorial	Yes
网络评论员	Internet commentators	Yes
网络监控	Internet monitoring	Yes

3. #sex# #drugs# #immorality#

CHINESE	ENGLISH	BLOCKED AS OF OCTOBER 2012?
一夜情	one-night stand	No
尤物	rare beauty	Yes
换妻	partner swapping	Yes
性交	sexual intercourse	Yes
作爱	make love	Yes

咪咪	meow / tits	Yes
六合彩	Mark Six lottery	Yes
露点	dew point / nipple slip	Yes
暴露	expose	No
春药	aphrodisiac	Yes
恋足	foot fetish	No
裸照	nude photograph	Yes
无毛	without hair	Yes
裤袜	panty hose	Yes
人吃人	cannibalism	No
女同	lesbian	No
七宗罪	seven deadly sins	Yes
近亲相奸	incest	Yes
大麻	marijuana	Yes
海洛因	heroin	No
白粉	white powder (heroin)	No
冰毒	methamphetamine	No
杜冷丁	Demerol	Yes
迷奸	roofied	Yes
射液	inject	Yes

4. #people#

CHINESE	ENGLISH	BLOCKED AS OF OCTOBER 2012?
徐勤先	Xu Qinxian	No
蒋彦永	Jiang Yanyong	No
三○一	301	No
温云松	Wen Yunsong	Yes
刘宾雁	Liu Binyan	Yes

彭丽媛	Peng Liyuan	Yes
习近平	Xi Jinping	Yes
邓颖超	Deng Yingchao	Yes
方励之	Fang Lizhi	Yes
馬明心	Ma Mingxin	No
刘荻	Liu Di	No
吴仪	Wu Yi	Yes
丁先皇	Dinh Bo Linh	Yes
冯正虎	Feng Zhenghu	Yes
李金	Li Jin (Kim Lee)	Yes
张筱雨	Zhang Xiaoyu	Yes
武藤兰	Ran Asakawa	No
文鲜明	Sun Myung Moon	Yes
王文怡	Wang Wenyi	Yes
费孝通	Fei Xiaotong	Yes
雷洁琼	Lei Jieqiong	Yes
黎智英	Jimmy Lai	No
密勒日巴	Milarepa	Yes
阿沛·阿旺晋美	Ngapoi Ngawang Jigme	Yes

5. #scandals# #disasters# #rumors#

CHINESE	ENGLISH	BLOCKED AS OF OCTOBER 2012?
倒台事件	downfall incident	Yes
万武义	Wan Wuyi	No
七五八大洪水	the Great Flood of August 1975	No
讣告	obituary	Yes
薄熙来	Bo Xilai	Yes
陈希同	Chen Xitong	Yes

我的奋斗	*Mein Kampf*	Yes
上蔡县	Shangcai	No
非正常死亡	unnatural death	Yes
富女	rich woman	Yes
退党	leave a political party	Yes
宋祖英	Song Zuying	Yes
锦州监狱	Jinzhou Prison	Yes
苏家屯	Sujiatun	Yes

6. #information# #media#

CHINESE	ENGLISH	BLOCKED AS OF OCTOBER 2012?
开放杂志	*Open Magazine*	No
遊行	parade	Yes
卫星电视	satellite television	Yes
卫星锅	satellite dish	Yes
罢工	labor strike	Yes
组织者	organizer	Yes
宪章	charter	Yes
推特	Twitter	Yes
毋忘	never forget	Yes
天安门母亲	Tiananmen Mothers	Yes
祖国母亲	Mothers of the Motherland	Yes
空凳	empty stool	No
快闪党	flash mob	Yes
自由花	"The Flower of Freedom"	Yes
三月学运	March Student Movement	Yes
茉莉花	jasmine flower	No
五四运动	May Fourth Movement	Yes

学生领袖	student leader	Yes
北高联	the Beijing Students Autonomous Federation	Yes
高自联	the Beijing Students Autonomous Federation	Yes
激流中国	*Dynamic China*	Yes
自由亚洲	Radio Free Asia	Yes
美国之音	Voice of America	Yes
独立中文笔会	Independent Chinese PEN	Yes
无国界记者	Reporters Without Borders	Yes
国际特赦组织	Amnesty International	No
博讯	Boxun.com	Yes

7. #security# #violence# #suppression#

CHINESE	ENGLISH	BLOCKED AS OF OCTOBER 2012?
坦克	tank	No
血案	massacre	No
屠杀	massacre	No
东方闪电	Eastern Lightning	Yes
便衣	plain clothes	No
迫害	persecution	No
九一一袭击	the September 11 attacks	No
封锁	blockade	Yes
砍刀	machete	Yes
窃听器	hidden microphone	No
喀什	Kashi / Kashgar	No
奥克托今	HMX	Yes
梯恩梯	TNT	Yes
血房地图	bloodstained housing map	Yes

伤口	wound	Yes
外泄	leak	Yes
东长安街	East Chang'an Avenue	No
中俄密约	Sino-Russian Secret Treaty	Yes
暴力拆迁	violent demolition	Yes
藏人抗议	Tibetan protest	Yes
钴-60	cobalt-60	Yes
空警200	KJ 200	Yes
煽动颠覆国家政权罪	inciting subversion of state power	Yes

8. #misc# #why?#

CHINESE	ENGLISH	BLOCKED AS OF OCTOBER 2012?
毛腊肉	hair bacon	Yes
三色猫	calico cat	Yes
加拿大法语	Canadian French	No
大法	Falun Dafa	No
伊斯兰	Islam	Yes
Hoobastank	Hoobastank	No
幸運☆星	*Lucky Star*	Yes
军阀	warlord	Yes
膏药旗	*gāoyàoqi* (the Japanese flag)	Yes
天葬	sky burial	Yes
敏感	sensitive	Yes
共狗	Communist dog	Yes
共匪	Communist bandit	Yes
赤匪	red bandit	Yes
毛匪	Mao's bandit	Yes

干你妈	dry (fuck) your mother	Yes
操你	grasp (fuck) you	Yes
草你妈	grass (fuck) your mother	Yes
支那	Zhina	Yes
溪蟹	river crab	No
洪家楼	Sacred Heart Cathedral	Yes
防洪纪念塔	flood control monument	Yes
彭博社	Bloomberg	Yes
驗證碼	CAPTCHA	Yes
亡国	conquered nation	Yes
维勒	Wöhler / Villar	Yes
增补	supplement	No
黑天使	black angel	Yes
色豹	color of leopard	Yes

ACKNOWLEDGMENTS

Much thanks to Mom and Norm. I am so lucky to have family like you to count on.

Thank you to the following for their support and feedback throughout—without them this would not have been possible:

Pierre F. Landry, Katherine Carlitz, instructors, friends, and the Asian Studies Center at the University of Pittsburgh; Xiao Qiang and the team at *China Digital Times*; Nathan Schneider, Eric Stoner, and Jasmine Faustino at *Waging Nonviolence* (an early version of the introduction first appeared on *WNV*); my editor Diane Wachtell, her assistants Jed Bickman and Kianoosh Hashemzadeh, Marc Favreau, Maury Botton, Sarah Fan, Fran Forte, and everyone at The New Press; Martin Johnson and GreatFire.org; fellow participants of the 2012 CUHK-Yale summer workshop; fellow classmates at IUP-Tsinghua; friends and family from 07003; Steven Holtzman; Josephine Landback; Ching-Wen Lee; Haan Lee and Jay Nelson; Audrea Lim; Shaolida; Hippo Wong and Sarah Chou; and many, many others.

PUBLISHING IN THE PUBLIC INTEREST

Thank you for reading this book published by The New Press. The New Press is a nonprofit, public interest publisher. New Press books and authors play a crucial role in sparking conversations about the key political and social issues of our day.

We hope you enjoyed this book and that you will stay in touch with The New Press. Here are a few ways to stay up to date with our books, events, and the issues we cover:

- Sign up at www.thenewpress.com/subscribe to receive updates on New Press authors and issues and to be notified about local events
- Like us on Facebook: www.facebook.com/newpress books
- Follow us on Twitter: www.twitter.com/thenewpress

Please consider buying New Press books for yourself; for friends and family; or to donate to schools, libraries, community centers, prison libraries, and other organizations involved with the issues our authors write about.

The New Press is a 501(c)(3) nonprofit organization. You can also support our work with a tax-deductible gift by visiting www.the newpress.com/donate.